YOUR FIRST MILLION WORDS

FINDING THE STORY INSIDE YOU

All the best!
Jeff [signature]

BOOKS BY JEFF WHEELER

Non-Fiction

Your First Million Words

The Grave Kingdom Series

The Cursed Fog
The Buried World
The Immortal Words

The Harbinger Series

Storm Glass
Mirror Gate
Iron Garland
Prism Cloud
Broken Veil

The Kingfountain Series

The Poisoner's Enemy (prequel)
The Maid's War (prequel)
The Poisoner's Revenge (prequel)
The Queen's Poisoner
The Thief's Daughter
The King's Traitor
The Hollow Crown
The Silent Shield
The Forsaken Throne

The Legends of Muirwood Trilogy

The Wretched of Muirwood
The Blight of Muirwood
The Scourge of Muirwood

The Covenant of Muirwood Trilogy

The Banished of Muirwood
The Ciphers of Muirwood
The Void of Muirwood

Whispers from Mirrowen Trilogy

Fireblood
Dryad-Born
Poisonwell

Landmoor Series

Landmoor
Silverkin

YOUR FIRST MILLION WORDS

FINDING THE STORY INSIDE YOU
JEFF WHEELER

AMBERLIN

Text copyright © 2019 Jeff Wheeler

All rights reserved.

No part of this book may be reproduced, or stored in a retrieval system, or transmitted in any form or by any means, electronic, mechanical, photocopying, recording, or otherwise, without express written permission of the publisher.

Published by Amberlin

ISBN-13: 9781696963916

Cover and Interior design by Steve R. Yeager

Printed in the United States of America

To Gina

CONTENTS

YOUR FIRST MILLION WORDS 2
GETTING INTO THE FLOW 6
DELICATE IDEAS 13
THE OGRE 20
CRUSTS AND LOAVES 28
REINVENTION 35
HAZCOM 42
THE HAN SOLO PRINCIPLE 48
PLOTS VERSUS CHARACTERS 53
IMPOSTER SYNDROME 61
FAILURE 69
INTEGRITY 81
JOHARI WINDOW 89
SEEING WITH NEW EYES 94
SHOULDERS OF GIANTS 100
FEEDBACK—THE PAINFUL GIFT 106
LOOK UP, THEN BACKWARD 115
WISDOM 121
POSSIBILITY THINKING AND
THE POWER OF POSITIVITY 126
PAIN'S PERSPECTIVE 135
A MANIFESTO ON VIRTUE 144
THE "GUH" MOMENT 147
UNFORESEEABLE 155
HOW TO SUCCEED 163

BOOKS ON THE CRAFT 171
BOOKS WITH BIG IDEAS 171
FAVORITE BIOGRAPHIES 172
ACKNOWLEDGMENTS 173

"A new idea is delicate. It can be killed by a sneer or a yawn; it can be stabbed to death by a quip and worried to death by a frown on the right man's brow."

—Ovid, Roman philosopher

YOUR FIRST MILLION WORDS

Each of us is meant to create. We have the wiring for it. Our minds are designed to do it.

Thomas S. Monson once wrote, "God left the world unfinished for man to work his skill upon. He left the electricity in the cloud, the oil in the earth. He left the rivers unbridged and the forests unfelled and the cities unbuilt. God gives to man the challenge of raw materials, not the ease of finished things. He leaves the pictures unpainted and the music unsung and the problems unsolved, that man might know the joys and glories of creation." We all have something itching inside of us, waiting to transform and come out. Ovid, a Roman philosopher and advisor to the emperor, wrote a book called *Metamorphoses*. It's a powerful word, and in one of my all-time favorite quotes from this work, Ovid says that new ideas are delicate and should be treated delicately because the sneer of another man might destroy the fragile thing before it's had the opportunity to transform. But other people aren't the only ones who stifle our creativity. So many of our germ ideas, the tiny, delicate ones, are killed off within the walls of our own *minds* before we give anyone else the opportunity to trample them.

That's what this book is about. Those nascent ideas we all have and how to protect them. From others. From ourselves. From being crushed by the day-to-day grind of life. This is a delicate dance I had to master in my journey as a writer.

The title of this book was inspired by a writing seminar I attended in 2004 that was taught by Terry Brooks, the fantasy author whose work kindled the writing flame inside me. He attributed a quote to Stephen King, though I've not found any interview or publication where he said it. Wherever the quote originally came from, the idea that was transmitted to me that I want to transmit to you is this: *After you've written your first million words, then you are ready to* start *being a writer.*

It takes a lot of mental resilience to sit in a chair and write a million words. It takes a long time. But I think there's a more important takeaway than the sheer difficulty of such an undertaking. The key word to me is "after." *After* you've written them. You see, it also takes incredible mental resilience to write the *next* million words. And then the next. As of this writing, I'm well on my way to four million.

After Terry Brooks's seminar, I was inspired to go home and count all the words I'd written up until that point, including five novels I wrote in high school, some novels I wrote during college, some more I wrote during my career at Intel, a number of short stories and novellas, and even a children's book. Using some old-fashioned estimating, I created a spreadsheet and tallied it up. It came to around 980,000 words. And that's when it hit me.

All those words were just practice.

I made the decision to throw them all away. Now, I'm not encouraging you to do the same with your first million words, but I had an epiphany after that writing seminar. Most of the words I'd written didn't deserve to be published. I'd reached a plateau, and it was time to start climbing again instead of trying to salvage parts from the scrap heap. The very next book I wrote was *The Wretched of Muirwood*. And that was the book that finally, eventually, helped me get published.

But I don't want to skip too far ahead.

Let's return to Ovid's point about the tenderness of ideas. Each of us has an inner critic, harsh and unrelenting. My own inner critic assured me that I was wasting my time trying to fulfill a teenager's fantasy of "being an author." But that voice didn't relent after my first books sold. Instead, it started telling me that I'd never be able to write anything half as good as Muirwood. That everything would go downhill from there. My best work was behind me. My royalties would evaporate, and I'd have to go find another job to pay the bills.

The more I've been involved in the business of creating things (whether they be microscopic microprocessors in multibillion-dollar wafer fabs, writing original music, or telling stories), the more I've heard echoes of this insidious voice coming from the heads of everyone else around me. Some call that voice Imposter Syndrome. Steven Pressfield called it Resistance. Napoleon Hill called it the Devil. Dorothea Brand called it the Will to Fail. Brené Brown calls it shame.

This book is about learning how to silence that voice so you can tap into the quiet whispers that come to a prepared mind and inspire things previously unimagined. Things that are good or worthwhile. Things that uplift. I've learned a lot about this other voice—this sacred voice—as a father, a husband, a teacher, a bishop, and a friend. This book is also the story of my personal journey as a writer and the lessons it has taught me, which I hope may be useful to others and encouraging to those who have chosen to pursue creative goals, whatever they may be.

This book has been squirming inside me like a caterpillar for many, many years. I told myself I'd finally sit down and write it after selling a million copies of my books. A million words, a million books . . . that would be perfect timing. Came and went. Then I picked a new milestone—I'd write the book as soon as one of my books hit the bestseller lists. That came and went too. A huge family move with all the accompanying upheaval and drama made me push it aside again, until I finally could repress the whispers no longer. It was time to let the magic from my books—the Medium, the Fountain, and the Knowing—guide me in a new direction. To heed the whispers from Mirrowen and follow where they led me.

Maybe it's time for you as well. Maybe you've been feeling it too. Life is busy, complicated, and complex. The time will never be right later.

And so I leave this introduction with a final thought from a French political philosopher. Jacques Bainville said (and I read the quote originally from Neal A. Maxwell) that "we must want the consequences of what we want."

So what do you want? And are you ready for the consequences?

GETTING INTO THE FLOW

Do you remember a time when you could spend hours, which felt like minutes, focusing on something creative? Maybe it was a drawing. Maybe it was just play. Maybe it was music. As children, we reach a state of mind called flow (see the research and brilliant TED talk by Mihaly Csikszentmihalyi) pretty easily. As children, we're so interested and engaged in what we're doing, hours can pass in an instant. I recall digging holes in my grandpa's backyard in Ogden, Utah, during summer vacation. At school, instead of playing soccer, I used to play pretend with two girls from my grade. I was always the Hulk, and they were usually horses or unicorns. We'd act out stories of our own creation. Recess flew by.

Where does your creative story start? What were the first tender shoots of creativity for you?

As I got older, I developed an interest in art. This first started, I think, at church, where a woman would draw pictures of Star Wars characters and ships for us kids. Art fascinated me, especially the idea of putting something on paper that existed in my mind. Or replicating an image someone else had done with all its detail. While I certainly wasn't the best artist at my school, I was voted by my peers in sixth grade as one of the two best artists in our class. It boosted my confidence at a time when I really needed it.

The writing spark lit for me in middle school. I enjoyed reading, but hadn't found any series that could measure up to Lloyd Alexander's Chronicles of Prydain, which I'd already read multiple times. But I kept trying other books, and one day at the library I picked up *The Elfstones of Shannara* by Terry Brooks. At the time, I didn't even realize it was the second book in the series. The cover art attracted me, so I picked it up. I thought I had it all figured out at the beginning, but Mr. Brooks threw all my theories into the garbage and took me on a tale of adventure and magic that I've never forgotten, full of surprises and unexpected setbacks.

It truly felt as if something were burning inside me—a match flaring to life. I couldn't stop reading. I stayed up way too late several nights in a row, and once, I even tried to wake up my younger brother (with whom I shared a room), needing to talk to someone about the story and explain why it was so intense. He groaned and wouldn't reply. By the time I finished the book, I was just *moved*. The ending was not what I'd expected, and the tension in the story wouldn't let go of me. The book had cast a spell on me, and I distinctly remember thinking, *Someday, I want to be able to write books that make others feel the way I'm feeling now.*

I took my first stabs at story writing in middle school, but I didn't save any of those first attempts, nor do I remember liking any of them. For me, it felt like trying to ride a bike for the first time—all awkwardness, imbalance, and falling over.

But I kept at it, trying to come up with new ideas to write about.

I was raised in Silicon Valley at the epicenter of the personal computer era, and my dad bought us a new Apple IIe for our home, giving me the tool I needed to get more serious about writing, something I vowed to do when I started high school that fall.

No one told me to write a novel. It wasn't an assignment—it was a passion. To pursue it, I had to sacrifice cartoon time, video game time, and time with my friends. I had to give up lesser priorities for a greater one. William W. Phelps wrote: "Sacrifice brings forth the blessings of heaven," something many of us have learned in pursuit of our dreams or goals.

When you sacrifice something important to you, it helps in the metamorphosis. I've learned this lesson again and again in my life. You have time to do the things that you prioritize the most. But that usually requires *not* doing something else.

That first novel was a thriller called *The Shadyrock Murderer*. It was a story about some teenagers caught up with a menacing ninja who was seeking revenge because of something that had been stolen during World War II. I used the program Word Handler and saved my chapters to floppy disks, which I kept in a beige plastic case and carried in my backpack so I could work on it both at school and at home. I learned to back up those disks after one of them became corrupted. After another episode or two like that, I learned to religiously back up my work so I wouldn't have to start over. To this day, I'm more than a little paranoid about having to rewrite something because of a data error and always keep multiple backup copies.

When I finished writing that fifty-page book, I was so proud of myself. I didn't have an audience. I had no readers. My parents weren't interested in reading it, and my siblings never made it far before quitting. But I'd had so much fun writing the novel and tweaking it that I wasn't ready for it to end. I envisioned a sequel so that I could expand the story of the characters I'd already created. Another problem to be solved. More danger to face. The second book came much faster than the first and was significantly longer. The story seemed to write itself.

Up in my bedroom, I would enter the same flow state I'd experienced as a small child playing in my grandfather's yard. I'd sit there for hours writing, creating. Envisioning worlds beyond the one in which I lived. I spent more time writing during summer vacation than I normally did. By the time I started my sophomore year, I felt pretty important, even though I was still invisible to most of my classmates. I was writing novels. I spent a lot of time living in my head and trying to come up with new plot ideas. My dad bought a dot matrix printer (super loud and scratchy) so that we could use the computer for homework, but I used it to print out copies of my books so I could edit them with a pen and then fix the changes on the computer later. It annoyed everyone in the family when I started printing copies of my books, as the printer would grind for hours at a time.

During math class one day, the girl who sat next to me asked me what I was doing with that stack of papers. She was one of the popular girls. I felt my cheeks flush, and I tried hiding the papers from her, but she persisted and asked what they were and why she kept seeing me working on them during class.

Bracing myself for her reaction, I told her that it was part of a novel I was working on.

Remember Ovid? *A new idea is delicate. It can be killed by a sneer or a yawn; it can be stabbed to death by a quip and worried to death by a frown on the right man's brow.* Or a teenage girl's brow in this instance.

Mercifully, her response was uplifting. She smiled, looked interested, and said, "That's cool. Can I read some?"

Yes, a new idea is delicate. But words can bolster someone as surely as they can crush them. A smile or single word of praise can motivate and nourish a tender shoot of creativity. It can protect or feed it.

How do you react when someone offers to share their creation with you? Do you look away from the screen in your hand? Do you meet their eyes? Do you smile? What if it's a friend who has written an awkward poem? Or someone who's started a song and isn't sure they like it?

What would have happened to me if that girl—whom I still remember and appreciate for her encouragement all these years later—had mocked me? Or said in a disdainful way that writing a book that wasn't even assigned in a class was totally lame, stupid, or silly?

I might not have had the courage to write my first million words. That story that she looked at (and then asked for more of the next day) was part of the million words I later threw away. Without the encouragement of one of my first readers, I might not have had the bravery to write the rest.

We all need someone to encourage our dreams, our passions.

Be that someone.

Be kind when someone shares a little piece of their soul with you.

"Care about what other people think, and you will always be their prisoner."

—Laozi, Chinese philosopher

DELICATE IDEAS

Looking back at your past—your childhood—do you see evidence that your first creative dream was crushed or killed? Did you shut your work away in a box after someone criticized it? Maybe it was a disapproving parent. A taunting classmate. The tools of ridicule and mockery have always been highly effective at stifling creativity. They are weapons, really.

My mother used to enjoy writing plays, until a classmate criticized her work. And then she stopped. Permanently. Perhaps something like this happened to you. It's important for all of us to recognize the role we play in responding to nonconstructive criticism. If we let cruel, crushing words infect our hearts, to fill us with doubt, discouragement, and shame, we are making a choice to do so.

If a sick person sneezed on you and you got sick, would you allow the infection to fester, or would you try to make yourself well? That answer seems obvious, doesn't it? Yet on a daily basis, we allow ourselves to be infected by the thought contagions of other people. We make permanent in our thinking something which should only be temporary. We have to be very careful what we let in and what we allow to stay. Our minds are like gardens. It's just as easy for weeds to grow as tomatoes and carrots. We are the gardeners. We have an obligation to pluck out the negative and encourage the positive. Yes, it's wonderful and inspiring when someone helps us along the way. But for the most part, we need to learn how to help ourselves.

You already know what inspired me to want to start writing and telling stories. You know that I sacrificed a nontrivial amount of time to do so. In the world of finance, they call this materiality. I heard that word a lot at Intel. It means something has a significant impact on something else and must be reported. In addition to writing, I also developed another hobby in high school that became "material" to my parents. That hobby was Dungeons & Dragons (D&D).

When I was a teen in the 1980s, it wasn't considered very cool to play D&D. It certainly wasn't something I talked about outside my friendship circles. Why? Fear of criticism. Funnily enough, the game is considered much cooler now that fantasy and sci-fi have become more mainstream in popular culture. My parents heard concerns that some D&D players got into devil-worshiping and cults, but I think they mostly considered it a big waste of time. Maybe all parents worry about their kids that way.

I enjoyed D&D because it was a platform for creating and telling stories. Think of it this way. I enjoyed *The Elfstones of Shannara* by Terry Brooks because of the excitement and action in the story. When the druid Allanon found himself trapped in Paranor by the baddie and his troupe of hissing catlike Furies, I could only go along for the ride and see how the author got him out of a situation. Within D&D, you can set up a similar conflict and think of a hundred different ways it might resolve. The players decide what to do and how to react. No matter what I thought of as dungeon master, I couldn't always predict what my friends, the players, would do. Playing the game was like *living* a book. I would take elements that inspired me from the stories I was reading and incorporate them into the campaigns I prepared as dungeon master. This allowed me to test my ideas out on my friends. It was a lot of fun, and being a dungeon master helped me improve my storytelling. I learned firsthand which plot twists worked, and which ones fell flat. My friends' excitement for more adventures kindled more ideas in my mind. And it was during these campaigns that I learned the art of the cliffhanger twists. I would always try to end a session at a spot that would drive them crazy with anticipation to play again, usually ending it with the words "that's all for tonight," which would cause outcries of angst and sometimes having things thrown at me.

Ultimately, this ended up serving as inspiration for my writing, especially in the first fantasy novel I wrote, *Landmoor*.

As I mentioned, all of these sessions led to some conflict with my parents. When I tried to explain the game was inspiring me to write stories that I could eventually publish, I was hit with a pretty common line of reasoning. I imagine you've heard it a time or two hundred if you're drawn to a creative profession. It goes something like this. *Only a scarce few people ever succeed in the publishing business* (or, if you will, insert any other profession). *Most people can't make a living doing that. Do you want to be a starving artist? You need to pick something practical, something that will help you provide for yourself and a family. The chances of being successful are so small. You'll never make it.*

Sound familiar? Many of us have heard these words, and some of us are probably guilty of having said them to someone else. Consider this—Walt Disney's father kept trying to force his son to stick with a job he hated for security. What if he'd agreed?

Each of us has a unique set of skills, interests, and passions. Most of us know what we're drawn to, what we're good at. We cannot allow someone else to do our thinking for us. As for those of us who have offered up this sort of advice—we run the risk of sentencing someone to a life of drudgery when we try to convince them to play it safe. Or that only certain careers have value. Or that every single person needs a college degree. People are not all the same, and there is not one correct path for everyone.

I've spent many years now studying the lives of people who have defied the odds and become successful in their chosen field, sometimes even *inventing* the field because it didn't exist at the time. In his book *Outliers*, Malcolm Gladwell talks about the ten-thousand-hour principle. That's how much practice it takes, on average, for someone to achieve mastery of a skill. It's not the actual number that's important, it's the concept of deliberate practice over an extended period of time. I've found the same to be true with writing a million words. Not every word counts, but it's the practice that matters, the deliberate attempt to improve. In order to devote this commitment of time to something, you need internal motivation and persistence. Those are the two key ingredients to finding success in any field. Without them, someone just won't put in the time necessary to become an expert.

Writing a novel isn't any harder than laying tile or building a barn. That doesn't mean every person can write a bestselling novel. It's all about having the desire and willingness to learn a craft and the grit to stick with it. For more on this, read Angela Duckworth's awesome book *Grit: The Power of Passion and Perseverance*.

We all have a choice to make. We're either going to let other people control our minds and infect us with *their* insecurities, *their* doubts, and *their* concerns, or we are going to have to take charge of our own minds. To basically set up a screen that keeps in the good and filters out the bad. Like landscaping fabric that lets water through but deprives the weeds of light so that only the plants you're cultivating have space to grow.

Not all parents and authority figures are determined to block the way to your goal. Perhaps you've heard this spiel from someone else—a spouse or significant other, friends, coworkers, members of your church and community, or backseat drivers on social media. Remember that it is *your* life to live, not theirs. Frankly, I'm glad Disney stopped listening to his dad. He kept drawing and went his own way and kept going, even after he failed multiple times.

Remember, you have to want the consequences of what you want. Most of us who have achieved success know that excelling at *anything* can be very lonely. Writing is a lonely profession. That's why authors, when they get together, can act quite strange.

My parents didn't convince me that my dream was impossible. Thankfully, I was born with a healthy dose of stubbornness. Or maybe it's just determination, but I think my wife and kids would agree it's a combination of both. Every time my parents launched into a speech about choosing a practical career, like an engineer or a professor, I would think in my mind, *Yeah, well, I'll show you. I'm going to be a full-time author someday.*

OK, so maybe it *is* stubbornness. But it's the same strain of stubbornness that drove the Wright brothers to invent a flying machine and figure out that the popular scientists of their day had the physics absolutely wrong (read David McCullough's excellent book *The Wright Brothers* for more). It's the same defiance that Andrew Carnegie, Bill Gates, Steve Jobs, Albert Einstein, and countless others tapped into to see beyond what was considered possible at the time.

Owning your own thoughts, your own mind, is so critical to achieving anything. I simply can't overstate the importance of this point. Of course, this is something that's easily said and not so easily done. Throughout my early adulthood, I remained doggedly committed to improving my craft and learning all that I could. But that's not to say I never came close to quitting.

In 2005, the book *Freakonomics* came out. I thought the authors, Steven D. Levitt and Stephen J. Dubner, were brilliant, and I relished the way they undermined popular wisdom regarding many contentious issues. Their arguments were totally convincing. And then I came across a passage that stopped me in my tracks. They compared the publishing industry (as well as a few other creative industries) to a tournament where people spend their lives vying for a spot that they eventually come to realize they will never get. And then they quit. I still have those passages underlined in my copy of the book.

My inner critic roared to life, of course, louder than ever. *See? Even the authors of* Freakonomics *think you're crazy! You will never get a book published by a* real *publisher. You will never succeed in this dream. You are wasting your time and your life. You should quit.*

That passage was a wake-up call for me. It was a test of my determination and resolve. And stubbornness. The temptation to quit was overpowering.

Never let someone else do your thinking for you. In a sense, the authors were right. The publishing industry in 2005 was pretty close to how they described it. But nothing stays the same. Industries evolve. Change is always around the corner. Determination is the only thing that will see you through.

Back to high school.

Now, I wasn't a fool. I knew my parents weren't wrong about everything—writing stories probably wouldn't pay the bills for a long time. So I decided that I should be a teacher. I didn't really like high school, per se, but it was all I really knew, and I knew I didn't want to work at a retail job forever. Being a teacher was an honorable profession, an acceptable career, and I'd never been frightened of public speaking. I loved telling stories and could imagine doing that in a classroom. It was a career that would give me time off during the summers to write and an opportunity to be surrounded by excellent source material (teenagers) for my stories.

Only that didn't work out either.

THE OGRE

I ended sophomore year with a broken ankle. I fell while spiking a ball in PE, and my ankle swelled up to the size of a baseball. I couldn't put any weight on it, so I ended up going to the ER. The X-ray revealed the extent of the injury, and I was soon fitted with a cast. Naturally, a lot of students wanted to hear about what had happened and to sign my cast. That, and the injury itself, put me behind at the very end of the semester.

It was a long-standing policy in my family that we had to earn a minimum of a B average. I was more interested in storytelling than academics, which was another reason my parents hated my D&D playing, but I'd managed to tightrope walk a 3.0 GPA during my first two years of high school. My grades slipped after the whole broken-ankle incident, however, and my English teacher gave me a dreaded C that final term, which put me at a 2.95. I hadn't met my parents' minimum expectations, and no amount of pleading, crying, or teen angst would soften my dad's heart. The punishment was that I had to pay for my car insurance beginning that summer.

I'm grateful that my parents held a hard line with me. It was exactly the push I needed to improve my grades. But I faced another consequence for getting that C in English—I was supposed to take a remedial English class. I absolutely did not want to do that because it meant I would be stuck taking the junior-level class during my senior year, which was when I had planned to take Writing for Publication and Creative Writing. I couldn't bear the thought of missing the only classes that actually excited me.

At the end of my sophomore year, when we put in our class requests for the next year, I defied my English teacher and put in for the junior-level class. I figured the worst thing that could happen was they'd catch the error and assign me to the remedial class. They didn't catch it, and I was assigned to Mr. Wilkinson's class. On the first day of class, he asked in a very grouchy voice whether any of us had gotten a C the previous year in English, because we weren't supposed to be there. I sat still, sick to my stomach, and was just rebellious enough to stay quiet. Now, I'm not advocating dishonesty. Perhaps if I'd talked to him after class, he might have allowed me to stay. I'm just saying what I did, which was keep my mouth shut.

At first, I thought I'd made a huge mistake because he made us memorize a ton of grammar facts. It felt as if I was in over my head, but I worked hard to memorize the facts and passed all the quizzes. That began to build my confidence. We then started writing essays in class, which I hated. Listening to some of my peers, however, I realized that a little creativity was rewarded. Mr. Wilkinson liked us to tickle our imaginations. For one essay assignment, I wrote a piece called "Love, the Amusement Park of Life." It was basically flash fiction with a

John Hughesian setting. Wilkinson loved it and gave it an A+. My classmates liked it too. That gave me the first small taste of having an appreciative audience. Wilkinson continued to be delighted by the other pieces I wrote for his class. His approbation instilled some much-needed confidence in me. It helped unleash my creativity in an academic setting.

It also gave birth to the ogre of author pride.

During that time I was still influenced by Brooks, but I was also reading some Dickens and a lot of Dave Barry, the humorist. I'd finished three thriller novels by this point and was running some major multi-episode D&D campaigns with my friends. My imagination was getting a regular workout. Another essay/short story earned more high marks, and I felt I was heading places. I decided to submit my first novel to Del Rey Books, even though they didn't publish thrillers. Having loved the Shannara series so much, I really wanted to see their logo on the spine of one of *my* books. I submitted it under a pen name, not wanting to reveal that I was just a high school student. After I submitted it, I thought publication would come easily. In my mind, I began to imagine a grandiose future where I wouldn't need to be a high school teacher at all. The ogre kept growing bigger and more ornery.

When I got my first rejection letter, it didn't deflate me at all. How many high school kids were submitting novels to New York? New ideas kept springing to life. The teacher of my business class assigned us to create our own country and its own political system and economy, something that was right up my alley. World building! I created an island nation called Armageddon, a place originally funded by the US government to train elite special forces. The soldiers had gone rogue, however, and decided to target their own enemies. That assignment inspired me so much that I wrote another thriller novel based on it, and I told my teacher about it. He was amazed the assignment had fostered such an idea and that I'd had the tenacity to actually write a book about it. I got an A in his class and had another novel under my belt. With that novel, I started putting edgier and edgier content in my writing. I was watching too much *Tour of Duty* (a military television series) at the time, I think. *Armageddon* was a kind of Shakespearean tragedy. I loved writing it, but it was pretty dark. The ogre pride within me smiled.

Finally, my senior year, I was able to take the two advanced writing classes that I'd been excited about since starting high school. My grades were stellar now, but my earlier lack of motivation limited what colleges I could attend in the future. I decided to go to a state university in the hopes that I could live at home to save money and find a decent-paying job in Silicon Valley. I hoped to work for Apple someday. My parents both wanted me to go to Brigham Young University (BYU) in Provo. But since I would have to pay for college myself, I felt that a state college was a better choice.

After high school, I intended to serve a mission for the Church of Jesus Christ of Latter-Day Saints, so I didn't want to start at the state college right away. Thankfully, there was a local community college nearby where I could take a few classes before leaving on my mission.

I enrolled in English 1A because it was a requirement before I could begin taking any of the creative-writing classes that I really wanted to take. I don't remember my teacher's name. But I remember, vividly, that I got a D on my first essay in his class.

I got that grade because what I'd written wasn't an essay. It was a short story.

That English 1A class taught me more about the ogre of author pride than anything else before or since. When we got the second essay assignment, the same thing happened. I believed, naively, that I could sway him to make an exception for me if I wrote a brilliant story that addressed the theme he wanted us to write about. He gave me an F that time. He also told me to come to his office hours and discuss my essay. I was so furious with him and sick to my stomach. I learned that high school isn't college. I learned that professors have standards, and when you fail to meet them, they give you the grade you deserve. It was one of my first lessons in the school of reality bites. Of the indisputable fact that actions have consequences. I told him (cheekily) that I was submitting novels to publishing houses in New York. He said that was wonderful. But in *his* class I needed to write essays, not stories. Later on, after I'd passed the basic English requirement, I could take all the creative-writing classes I wanted. He humbled me.

I struggled writing essays in that class. It was totally demotivating to me. I hated the books we read too. Our in-class discussions of those books were difficult to endure. I had to rewrite nearly all of my essays multiple times, conforming my mind to the structure and format he required. In the end, I worked hard and got a C in that class. And I knew that I would probably have to take it over again once I enrolled at the state college.

For the time being, the ogre was conquered. Thirty hit points of damage. Critical hit. Boom.

I went on my mission and did a lot of growing up over the next two years. Until then, I'd never lived outside of California, but my mission brought me to Oklahoma and Texas, where the culture, population, geography, and (especially) meteorology were remarkably different from Silicon Valley. It was humbling to realize I only knew a small corner of our big world, and even more humbling to face the repeated failures endured by every missionary. I continued to have creative ideas but didn't have the chance to do anything more than scratch a few notes in my journal.

When I started college at the state college in the fall of 1992, I took English 1A again. My first essay earned an A. So did the second. I knew more about human nature by then, more about how the world worked and how it enforced consequences. I had also learned to see outside myself. To observe others and try to see from their point of view. My English 1A professor told me that I shouldn't even be in his class. He praised my essays and encouraged me, at the end of the term, to skip English 1B completely. In fact, he explained the process of how I could test out of it after only attending the first three classes. Following his advice, I was able to drop English 1B.

It was in Mr. Jerry Hannah's creative-writing class where I learned the phrase "beware the ogre of author pride" for the first time. It resonated with me then and still does.

Pride is kryptonite. It is the antithesis of the creative voice—indeed, it drowns it out. And the problem is that it poisons unpublished authors as surely as it does successful ones. It bloated my ego during high school and then came crashing down on me in English 1A.

So much of our journey happens inside our own heads. We blame others because it's too painful to blame ourselves. What fables do we tell ourselves about reality? Napoleon is claimed to have said, "What is history but a fable agreed upon?" Our own "histories" are compiled in our minds, the stories about ourselves and how we got to where we are.

If you want to succeed in any endeavor, especially creative ones, you need to learn to strip yourself of the ogre of pride. And it's a constant effort, one that will take the rest of your life. It is part of our nature as human beings. John Adams said, "A desire to be observed, considered, esteemed, praised, beloved, and admired by his fellows is one of the earliest as well as the keenest dispositions discovered in the heart of man."

Some have it worse than others. I have a healthy share of it myself, which I've fought against my whole life. That's why I'm grateful to that first English 1A teacher.

The life lesson he gave me has paid dividends.

"In reality, there is, perhaps, no one of our natural passions so hard to subdue as pride. Disguise it, struggle with it, beat it down, stifle it, mortify it as much as one pleases, it is still alive, and will every now and then peep out and show itself; you will see it, perhaps, often in this history; for, even if I could conceive that I had compleatly overcome it, I should probably be proud of my humility."

—Benjamin Franklin, publisher

CRUSTS AND LOAVES

When I look back at my college years, sometimes I can't believe everything that was squeezed into one day. Gone were the weeks where I could play D&D after school for hours on end. Something I've since taught my kids is that the ratio of free time to work time shifts throughout your life. When you become an adult, the amount of free time shrinks rapidly to balance extra time spent on obligations. That's just part of life, which means that the older you get, the more you have to learn to prioritize.

Let me try to paint the picture for you.

Following my two-year mission for The Church of Jesus Christ of Latter-Day Saints in Oklahoma, I enrolled in state college as a history major to pursue my goal of becoming a teacher. But in the meantime, I needed a summer job to help fund my living expenses and tuition.

During my mission, I had spent six months in the mission office, training in different office-place applications. When I went to a temp agency, this experience, plus my ability to type eighty words per minute, helped me land a job at the training department of Intel. Called Intel University, it was part of Human Resources. This was in 1992, before Intel had become the number-one semiconductor company in the world.

I'd only expected to work there through the summer, but they asked if I could stay on part-time during the school year. I was ecstatic. It wasn't Apple in Cupertino, but it was still a great opportunity. The job was flexible, and it allowed me to work and save up money while attending school. But the longer I worked at Intel, the more my hours crept up, and I started taking as many night classes as I could to work more during the day.

By 1994, I was married to my wife, and we lived in a duplex near the university. While she graduated college that year and began working full-time, I continued my studies. Since I much preferred the university environment to high school, I had decided to become a history professor rather than a high school teacher. That meant getting a PhD in history, but I wasn't deterred—my new goal fit in with my long-term goal of becoming a writer. My boss at Intel was supportive, as she'd been a history professor prior to joining the company.

Through all of this, the writing bug kept biting me hard. I had papers to write and tons of homework every week, but I set aside time on Saturdays for some creative writing and kept working on a historical-fiction novel that I'd been daydreaming about for years. After finishing it, I decided to try my first fantasy novel and wrote the first draft of *Landmoor*, based on my D&D campaigns from high school and beyond (my friends and I had started up again after I returned from my mission). It was intended to be an epic fantasy series spanning a dozen books, based on all the different adventures and plots I'd created as dungeon master. When I was writing, time seemed to disappear. I could easily spend all day writing and never lose motivation, but I knew that would damage my relationship with my wife, so we agreed on a fixed amount of time. I looked forward to writing every week. But homework had to come first. I was also grateful that my temp job at Intel had turned into a permanent "blue badge" position (part-time). Benefits, holidays, and vacation days were luxuries I'd never had before.

But life never sits still. At least not for very long.

A year after getting married, my wife and I were asked to become seminary teachers. For those not familiar with our faith, seminary is a program for high school teenagers. Each year the curriculum is the scriptures. We agreed to teach the Old Testament to a large class of freshmen, with a few sophomores, at six o'clock in the morning, five days a week. Some may wonder why my wife and I accepted such a demanding responsibility. We both had faith that our leaders had been inspired to choose us, knowing that we were still newlyweds, college students, and working nearly full-time. And we had made the commitment, years before, to put God first in our lives.

We did the best we could, and that first class gave us a lot of experience in dealing with the classroom. Some of the lessons flopped big-time. Some are still memorable, like the time we decided to record a video of the kids acting out the capture of King Zedekiah after the fall of Jerusalem. In the account in 2 Kings 25, Zedekiah has his eyes put out after watching his children being executed before him. The kid who played Zedekiah got two ketchup packets and squeezed them into his eyes to add some gory detail to the program (his idea, not ours). The ketchup began to sting, and so the pain he displayed wasn't all acting.

This new commitment added another layer of stress to our lives, for now we had to come up with daily lessons to try to engage the minds and hearts of sleepy teenagers. I still remember one night, around eleven p.m., when we were trying to prepare the next morning's lesson after a long and exhausting day. It felt as if we were at the ends of our ropes, emotionally and physically. My wife fell asleep, and I didn't have the heart to wake her. The lesson I prepared was on the story of Elijah and the widow (1 Kings 17). There was a great famine in the land, and Elijah was instructed to go to Zarephath, where a widow had been commanded to sustain him with food. When he got there, he found the widow. She was about to make a final meal for herself and her son out of a handful of meal and a little bit of oil and then die of starvation. The prophet asked her to "make me thereof a little cake first."

As I read that scripture, I felt heat and energy fill my chest. The widow did as she was asked, knowing it would be the end of her, and a miracle happened. Her barrel of meal never emptied, and her cruse of oil didn't fail until after the famine ended.

The story made me realize that I'd reached the end of my own barrel, so to speak. I had given all that I had to give of my time and energy. There were so many commitments, I felt pulled in every direction. I needed to trust God to replenish me. My despair turned to hope, and I realized that I wasn't alone. My wife and I were like the widow in the story—the sacrifices we were making were not going unnoticed. It was a tender moment, a personal connection with God, as I realized the message had been sent to me in the exact moment when I most needed it. The fatigue left me at once, and I finished the lesson. I shared the experience with my wife the next morning, and it renewed our determination to give the seminary classes our best effort. Both of us felt strengthened and reinvigorated.

I had been reminded of a lesson I'd first learned as a middle schooler writing novels on my family's Apple IIe. When life gets busy, you have to shift your focus to what's most important. There's an acronym I learned at Intel—ZBB—which encapsulates this concept perfectly. The acronym means "zero-based budget," but the principle is that you have fixed resources, usually smaller than you want, and that you need to prioritize on doing the most important things, not all the things you *want* to do. When something falls below the ZBB line, you don't do it anymore.

But when we have deep obligations (work, school, church responsibilities), we have to set some of our wants on the altar. When we do this, God empowers us to accomplish more than we thought we could. So for those who would wonder why we accepted such responsibility in the first place, again, it was because we felt it was what God wanted us to do. When we put God first in our lives, we're entitled to His help.

In researching the lives of other authors, I came to learn that many of them dedicated upward of eight hours a day writing. But I taught myself to disregard those benchmarks. I couldn't hold myself accountable for the time it took other people to get things done. Just because I didn't have huge sums of time myself didn't mean I couldn't write. I learned to ZBB (or sacrifice) from things that offered less value for my time, like television shows and movies. I realized, during those years of time famine, that if I wanted to achieve my dream of writing books, I needed to spend more time being creative than I did being entertained.

When we sacrifice for others, putting their needs and lives ahead of our own, that act is honored. God empowers us to accomplish more than we thought possible, and blessings we didn't anticipate will surface in our lives. Although my wife and I didn't have much time, we both had jobs with benefits. We had no problem paying rent or setting aside savings. And although I didn't have much time to write, I did have my creative-writing assignments for college and regular writing sessions once a week. Those were all great blessings.

Years later, when I was asked to take on another really challenging assignment at church, I heard it put this way by one of our leaders, "A person cannot give a crust to the Lord without receiving a loaf in return."

In the end, the things I sacrificed did not seem so very great. I don't regret *not seeing* more television shows. Or movies. But there are plenty I *do* regret having seen because of the the utter waste of time.

Examine your own life. What were you put on this earth to accomplish? To achieve? How are you going to ensure you have enough time to practice the skills you will need to master to succeed? All of us have more flexibility than we think we do. Sometimes our habits are just things we've grown accustomed to over the years. What time you get up in the morning. What time you go to bed. How much you read. What you eat. How often or whether you exercise. These are all habits. Habits are hard to change, but you can change them. I suggest that you do a little ZBB experiment to find out how you are spending your time, and how you can fit in what matters most to you.

With any activity, whether it's making pancakes or fixing a faucet, you'll make plenty of mistakes on the first few tries. The fantasy novel I was writing back then wasn't originally called *Landmoor*. The working title was *Elven Pride*. And it was right as I was finishing it that I realized books about elves just weren't selling to publishers anymore. There were too many elves, from Tolkien to Brooks to Feist, to the Dragonlance Saga by Hickman and Weis. It was a staple in the genre. One that was overused.

A sickening feeling told me that if I stuck with elves, I wasn't going to find a publisher. The book I'd just finished was told from the point of view of a young elven man!

I realized with dread that my first pancake might be a flop.

REINVENTION

Another insightful line of scripture I learned teaching seminary that first year was: "There is no new thing under the sun." (Ecclesiastes 1:9). Consider this the next time someone tells you that your idea isn't unique: Tolkien didn't invent the elves. They existed in mythology long before him. What he did was *reinvent* them. Brooks may have borrowed some ideas from Tolkien in regard to elves in *Sword of Shannara*, but he reinvented the whole concept in *Elfstones of Shannara*, my favorite book. Stephenie Meyer didn't invent vampires. Instead, she helped bring paranormal romance to the masses.

Just about every author I've studied or met was inspired by someone else. A medieval philosopher, Bernard de Chartres, wrote that we are all like dwarves standing on the shoulders of giants. Our perspective is only possible because of the great people who came before us. Isaac Newton, rephrasing the sentiment, said, "If I have seen further, it is only by standing on the shoulders of giants."

As you already know, Terry Brooks inspired me. But who inspired him? Mr. Brooks told me himself that he was inspired by William Faulkner. C. S. Lewis was inspired by George MacDonald. William Shakespeare had inspiration from Ovid, among others. When I set out to write my novels, I didn't want to *be* the next Terry Brooks. When I first started, I would sometimes ask myself how Terry would have written a particular sentence. Described this or that idea. I struck a dead end every time. Each writer needs to find his or her own voice. But that doesn't mean every single author who writes about elves needs to reinvent every detail about them.

The problem with tropes is the baggage accompanying them. Sometimes this baggage can be good and helpful. For example, most readers have a good mental image of various medieval tropes (knights, kings, castles), which can lift some of the burden of explaining every detail of these things within a story. But other tropes (elves, dwarves, magic rings, fire-breathing dragons) have been done so many times that readers cringe unless you make them *new*.

I realized I had a problem with my first fantasy novel, *Elven Pride*. The very title of the book screamed cliché. I still wanted to use my protagonist, but I didn't want to feed into readers' expectations of what elves were and did. The idioms go something like this: elves have long ears, high moral fiber, a remarkable affinity for magic and bows, and they live longer than humans. Although I didn't want to reinvent every aspect, I wanted to put my own spin on it and invite the reader to learn some new rules. I hoped to challenge them.

I changed the name from *elves* to the Shae. But a new name is only a cosmetic change—it's not enough. The Shae, I decided, carried recessive genes they passed on to their posterity (light-colored hair, limited eye colors). Pale skin as well, something I was familiar with since I'd been teased in high school for looking like Boo Radley from *To Kill a Mockingbird*. Although elves are typically depicted as deeply honorable, above the petty matters of other beings, the Shae were in the mire with everyone else. Their trading practices were predatory, and they'd developed a bad reputation for dishonesty among their neighbors. Instead of giving them pointy ears, I chose to highlight another trait—their eyes—which glowed in the dark the way a cat's eyes reflect the light. And yes, they had an affinity for magic in all its forms, but their culture had prohibitions against certain kinds of magic (like their own form of the Mosaic Law from the Old Testament).

As I was rewriting the book to update the world building, I noticed I'd included too many point-of-view characters. The constant changes in perspective sucked tension out of the story and slowed the plot. This was aggravating to realize. It meant I had to rewrite it yet again to remove one of the point-of-view characters (Exeres), whom I decided to introduce in the sequel instead.

All in all, I rewrote or revised that novel *seven* times over a period of many years. Besides the changes I've mentioned, I tweaked the opening over and over again, knowing it was too slow and tedious. This was something I'd gleaned after taking one of my college-level creative-writing classes, for which I submitted elements from *Landmoor* (the revised title). I would often get so disgusted with it I'd put it away for months. I just didn't have the stomach to keep working on it and would venture onto other projects. Translating a D&D adventure into a novel was more difficult than I'd thought it would be, but in my heart I still believed it could become an epic fantasy series that would run for a dozen or more books. There was enough plot in my head to accomplish this goal—which was, perhaps, part of the problem. Since it was based on my old D&D campaigns with my friends, each of the characters had an arc. I'd savored the challenge of knitting these arcs together, but I was starting to realize the story was overcrowded. The more time I spent with it, the more I realized something still wasn't working, but I'd invested so much time in it that I couldn't conceive of abandoning it. I believed if I just persisted in making enough revisions, it would work.

Reinvention is still a principle I use today in my writing. Before I wrote my Harbinger Series, I daydreamed about writing a Dickensian novel. I've loved Dickens since high school and have grown to love Austen, the Brontë sisters, Gaskell, Trollope, and many others. But again, there are so many established tropes associated with the Regency era, such as elegant balls, rich young bachelors, carriages, and the filth of London. I still wanted to write in that era, but I knew I had to make it different. I also knew that many others who wrote Regency fantasy novels had already done a lot of work in this space. Would it be too cliché?

The idea came to me that instead of re-creating Regency England, I could invent my own version of it based on one of my existing fantasy worlds. I took tropes that would be expected (think Pemberley from *Pride and Prejudice*) and thought, Why not make the manors float on enormous rocks? That necessitated changing the mode of transportation from carriages to something that could fly, and so I dreamed up sky ships that could operate under the magic of the Medium from my Muirwood world so that I wouldn't have to use steampunk magic (i.e., hot-air balloons) to get people from place to place.

I chose to save the reveal—that the world was Muirwood—for the end of book one by renaming the magic, calling it the Mysteries. It would operate in the same way, but its powers would have grown and developed in the interceding centuries.

What is wonderful to me about this process of reinvention is that it can be repeated over and over again. It's a basic tool each writer should have in their toolbox.

What author has inspired you? Have you analyzed their work critically? How did they reinvent their genre? How can you do this in your own way? (I.e., What elements do you want to keep? What will you change?)

For me, this is part of the writing process that I really enjoy. At first, it was something I turned to in desperation *after* I'd written a novel. How much time would I have saved if I'd done it first? Carpenters like to say "measure twice, cut once." But as I like to say, experience is the best teacher.

Rewriting *Landmoor* ad nauseam was a critical part of my first million words. Perhaps that's one of the reasons why I don't want to write in that world anymore. I can also see all the flaws that I was blind to during my long cycle of writing and rewriting.

Making connections between what worked in the past and what might work in the future can't happen, however, if you aren't constantly sprinkling fertilizer on your mind. It's an aphorism now to say to new writers that they must read, read, read, and *then* write.

But what should you read? How do these baptisms of thought happen?

It requires, I'm afraid, another tedious skill you should develop if you haven't already.

Concentration.

"Concentration is my motto—first honesty, then industry, then concentration."

—Andrew Carnegie, philanthropist, steel tycoon

"Whatever luck I had, I made. I was never a natural athlete, but I paid my dues in sweat and concentration and took the time necessary to learn karate and become world champion."

—Chuck Norris, the one and only

HAZCOM

For many creative people, school can be a real trial when there are countless more interesting things to do. For me, school was often mind-numbingly tedious. I didn't want to sit and listen to lectures unless the teacher said something I found interesting. Those of you who have read the Harbinger novels may remember that one of the heroines, Sera, had a similar difficulty. Now you know why! I was probably the quintessential Calvin from the comic strip *Calvin and Hobbes*. I really enjoyed most of my history and English classes, but I struggled with geometry, chemistry, and foreign languages.

One of the main reasons I struggled was because I hadn't worked on the ability to concentrate. For me, writing didn't require much concentration because I would enter a flow state, and time would zip by. But that's the whole thing about flow—it requires a certain level of interest. It's hard to achieve flow when you couldn't care less about the Pythagorean theorem or why optical inhomogeneities in transparent materials are called by the German name *schlieren*. Frankly, I'm still not sure why that word has stuck with me this long.

The ability to concentrate is, I think, one of the prerequisites of finding success in any field. Nothing is stopping you from practicing this. It's another step in disciplining your mind to come up with your first million words. This chapter is about my journey in learning to exercise this skill, shared in the hope that it might inspire yours.

I first began to develop the ability to concentrate during my two-year mission. Every morning, we did personal study and companionship study. Some of those mornings, it took all the mental fortitude I could muster to stay awake. Studying Isaiah that early in the morning can have a powerful chloroform effect. But I kept at it and came to enjoy that study time and what I learned in it. I began to see the stories within the scriptures. To discover the connections between them. To learn little phrases full of wisdom and understand them. Doesn't Jesus say, *Seek, and ye shall find?* The process of seeking can be pretty dull and painstaking. But it taught me how to concentrate. To fix my mind on a task and stick with it to the end, even if it was boring.

I would need that steadfastness when I got to Intel. Some of my first duties there proved to be incredibly boring. One assignment was to input instructor scores from paper surveys into a computer. It was raw data entry, and no one at Intel University *wanted* to do it, so they gave that job to the temp (me). Another really tedious task was babysitting the HAZCOM class. HAZCOM is short for "hazardous communications," which was one of the mandatory safety courses required of anyone hired to work inside D2, Intel's research and development factory (fab). This class was self-directed, so I essentially had to sit in the back of the room for four hours to make sure no one left. But the benefits of the job far outweighed the tedium of these tasks—so I stuck with it.

Jenkin Lloyd Jones once said: "Anyone who imagines that bliss is normal is going to waste a lot of time running around shouting that he's been robbed. The fact is that most putts don't drop. Most beef is tough. Most children grow up to be just ordinary people. Most successful marriages require a high degree of mutual toleration. Most jobs are more often dull than otherwise. . . . Life is like an old-time rail journey—delays, sidetracks, smoke, dust, cinders, and jolts, interspersed only occasionally by beautiful vistas and thrilling bursts of speed. The trick is to thank the Lord for letting you have the ride."

I've since learned that willpower is finite (see Roy F. Baumeister and John Tierney's awesome book *Willpower* for the science behind it), meaning it can be both depleted and replenished. But it's also like a muscle—your capacity for it will increase over time if you continually exercise it. Aristotle once said, "Excellence is an art won by training and habituation. We do not act rightly because we have virtue or excellence, but we rather have those because we have acted rightly. *We are what we repeatedly do. Excellence, then, is not an act but a habit.*" [Italics added.] Various things helped me build up that muscle. College was one of them.

My college experience involved a lot of reading outside of class. The professors and teachers were all quite good, some better than others, but there were always textbooks and assigned readings to plow through. After sitting in class for hours, then working at Intel for hours, I would then have to trudge through pages of homework. This inspired me to learn a better and more efficient way of processing the material—

what I call economy of effort. Whenever I read something for school, I always a kept a pen or pencil handy to highlight sentences that jumped out at me as interesting or important. Gems I found within the text. Later, when studying for a test, I'd focus on those mental flags, which would help me recall the important highlights of the piece.

I practice this habit to this day, using the highlighter and notes feature on my apps to serve the same purpose, but I also jot notes in the margins of my books. It's given me a quasi-photographic memory over the years. Sometimes I can recall the location of the note I'm looking for (if, for example, it's on the top right side of the page), so I can flip through the book and find it faster.

To build my concentration muscle, I also pushed myself to connect the material I was learning with my existing body of knowledge—putting them together like jigsaw puzzle pieces. For example, when I wrote essays in college, I always tried my best to find ways to connect those essays to topics that intrinsically interested me. This helped me remember the information later.

It also helped, later on, to realize that no matter how boring HAZCOM was for *me*, it was critically important to the new techs who'd been hired to work in the clean room. While testing the pH of a can of Coke isn't inherently dangerous, working with hydrofluoric acid is a different story. It wasn't until a few years later, in 1997, when I started working for the D2 factory as a night shift supervisor, that the dangers of HAZCOM really came to light. Five years after "babysitting" the HAZCOM classes as a temp employee, I found myself back at HAZCOM as a student. Thankfully, I already knew all the answers by then.

And while the writing itself still comes naturally to me—bringing me back to that delicious flow state—it doesn't all come easily. Concentration and patience are vital in the research phase. My Kingfountain books, for example, are steeped in Arthurian lore. I purchased translations of medieval Arthurian tales like the *Mabinogion* and the Post-Vulgate Arthuriad and read book after book, story after story, in all their mind-numbing details. Thankfully, I continue to exercise that willpower muscle, and I can read a boring book without becoming bored or distracted. The benefit comes when I find a detail that inspires an element of the series I'm writing. I gleaned seeds of ideas for my Harbinger Series from Charles Dickens's *Bleak House*, for example. I love Dickens, but he can run on for page after page with insignificant details that could use some pruning according to our modern sensibilities. But back then, without other forms of entertainment to distract, Dickens could get away with such digressions. Modern technology has made it harder for us to maintain such focused concentration, but it is very important to develop this ability if you want to succeed in almost any field.

One of my all-time favorite characters that I've written is Ankarette Tryneowy from *The Queen's Poisoner*. Readers have seemed to connect with her as well. The idea of her came from an obscure historical text I read in college while working on my history degree. Decades later, I was able to pinpoint the quote that inspired the idea along with the scribbles in the margins. Even her name was inspired by that research. If you're interested, do a little research on Ankarette Twynyho for more information on the late-fourteenth-century woman who was executed by the Duke of Clarence (illegally, I might add) for poisoning his wife.

THE HAN SOLO PRINCIPLE

The inspiration for the Twilight Saga came to Stephenie Meyer in the form of a dream. It was a scene from her first book, the one in which Edward confirms to Bella that he's a vampire. In her dream, Ms. Meyer witnessed the conversation between the two characters, each revealing something about themselves by the way they talked and communicated.

My first published story, "The Wishing Lantern," was also inspired by an imagined conversation. The two characters were named Hickem Tod, an anthropomorphic frog called a ferzohg—if you didn't notice, every other letter spells F-R-O-G—and Estellionata, a snobby shimmer faerie trapped in a magic lantern. He's tall, quiet, and wise; and she's tiny, cranky, and explosive. The dialogue between them just jumped off my fingertips, and it felt as if the story wrote itself. It all poured out of me in a flow state one afternoon.

Conversation reveals us to each other, in life and in fiction. It's why we love to read banter, like the witty repartee between Emma and Mr. Knightley in Jane Austen's matchmaking classic *Emma*. Characters come to life when they're interacting with other characters. So often, I read novels or short stories where a single point-of-view character narrates the whole thing without interacting with anyone else for a long portion of the story. The character is alone—solo. Boring. Even Tom Hanks, brilliant as he is, couldn't have carried *Cast Away* if he hadn't had a very important costar: a volleyball named Wilson. There needs to be dynamic tension between people. Or a person and a volleyball, as the case may be. Hence the Han Solo principle.

I loved *Star Wars* as a kid and not just for the special effects. It was watching Han Solo banter with Luke and Leia that kept me coming back. That dynamic tension between characters is what drew me to the movie and to this idea, while I also admit I chose it because it's a fun play on words. It was Bella and Edward's long, tense conversations that kept people reading the Twilight Saga. That's why to me, the most important part of the storytelling process is coming up with the cast first. Who will be on stage? How will they argue or mess with each other? Who is the villain, and how will they throw wrenches in the spokes? It's all about people, and the more relatable they are, the more readers will grab on.

I wrote "The Wishing Lantern" for my creative-writing class in college, and the professor gave the story an A+ and wrote above the title, "This would make an excellent children's story." I asked him if he thought the story could be publishable. Let's just say the ogre of author pride had been humbled a bit by that point. He thought it could, yes. With his encouragement, I began submitting it to magazines and publishers across the country. I wasn't as cocky that time. Imagine my surprise and wonder when I got a response from PKA's *Advocate* accepting the story.

That was the first time something I'd written had gone out to the world. I still have a copy of that treasure. It was another stepping-stone along the journey. I think writing short stories is a great training for authors practicing the craft. One isn't expected to have the same plot complexity or world building in a short story, and it is also easier to practice all the fundamental elements of a story (beginning, middle, end) in a shorter time window. Before I wrote *Landmoor*, I tried writing short stories set in that world. It was good practice.

When I review short stories submitted to my e-zine *Deep Magic*, one of the first things I consider is whether the narration is all about the main character. Are they telling us directly who they are and what they want? If so, I tend to lose interest quickly. We don't see ourselves very objectively anyway. We reveal much more of ourselves in how we talk, how we move, how we argue, how we listen. Characters need others to bounce off of, like elements that interact and form new chemical bonds. The whole is worth more than the sum of its parts.

One source of inspiration for me has been the stories of real-life people. I love reading biographies, and one thing I've learned from them is that none of the greats in our world found success on their own. They had rivals. There were strained relations with family and friends. They encountered personal setbacks. All of these are fodder for creating believable characters.

Some of my favorite biographies are Andrew Carnegie's autobiography; Walter Isaacson's books on Benjamin Franklin, Einstein, Steve Jobs, and Leonardo Da Vinci; Ron Chernow's books on Alexander Hamilton and Rockefeller; any book about Abraham Lincoln (David Herbert Donald's and Doris Kearns Goodwin's are two of my favorites); and just about anything from David McCullough. I also enjoy reading more obscure historical biographies like *Boyd* by Robert Coram, where I learned about the OODA (observe, orient, decide, act) loop that military strategists use today, and *The Black Count* by Tom Reiss, which tells the true story of Alexandre Dumas's father, a man who inspired the kind of stories his son wrote about.

If a historical figure catches my interest, I'll usually start with Wikipedia to get a quick overview of their life, then I'll buy some books from the references to get a deeper look at the person's story. I read several biographies, for example, about Mary Tudor while researching the Covenant of Muirwood Trilogy. She was my main inspiration for my heroine, Maia, and many little details about her life ended up in my novels—especially how she interacted with others who tried to force her to change her religion. I also read *The Perfect Prince* by Ann Wroe about the prince "imposter" who claimed to be the heir to the English throne, to harvest details of his life and marriage, which I used in the plots for the second and third Kingfountain books. *China's First Emperor and His Terracotta Warriors* by Frances Wood and the Crane-Iron Pentalogy by Wang Du Lu helped ignite ideas for my Grave Kingdom Series.

Another place to look for believable characters are the people around you. Sometimes I borrow a name, a personality, an idiosyncrasy—occasionally all three—for my characters. Some of these people know they are in my books. Most do not, especially if I have them playing the role of a villain. The point, again, is to flesh out your main characters by how they interact with others, rather than having them describe themselves. Show, don't tell (there's a reason so many people say this).

Another trick I use is to borrow a side character from some classic piece of literature or film and transport that person into one of my worlds to interact with the main character. In *Blight of Muirwood*, for example, I introduce a character named Martin, the new hunter of Muirwood Abbey. This character was inspired by Captain Fluellen in Shakespeare's *Henry V*, the Kenneth Branagh version. I even studied the text of the play to focus on his very few lines of dialogue to see how Shakespeare had made him so memorable to me. That's where I found his "by Cheshu" line, which he uses over and over. Martin's job is to help the heroine, Lia, see an essential truth about herself.

Of course, none of this is to say that you should give several characters a point of view in your book or story. As I mentioned earlier, this was something I needed to change in *Landmoor*. The point of the Han Solo principle is that your point-of-view character should begin, very quickly, to interact with secondary characters. This is the best way to reveal who your hero or heroine is—and to reveal the natures of the people around them.

Joseph Smith once said, "I am like a huge, rough stone rolling down from a high mountain; and the only polishing I get is when some corner gets rubbed off by coming in contact with something else, striking with accelerated force . . ."

That's how characters get made. By colliding with each other.

It is in the collision of people that true character is revealed.

PLOTS VERSUS CHARACTERS

Stories from real life don't come in nice little packages with predictable outcomes and endings. While some readers might complain that a plot point feels contrived, I've learned from reading biographies and histories that unexpected twists happen in real life. In fact, the deeper you dig into the past, the more you realize that most great stories hinge on one essential factor going right (or wrong, as the case might be). One example of this is during the American Revolutionary War. General Washington's army was about to be outflanked and defeated by the British army. The realization came too late, however—they didn't have time to make it. Suddenly, a fog bank rolled in, providing life-saving cover and allowing his army to slip away and escape certain death. In another incident, which inspired an important moment in my second Kingfountain Series, a bolt of lightning struck the emperor's palace in Beijing, which burned down the city and prompted the emperor to recall his fleet of treasure ships from exploring the known world.

These were both deus ex machina situations. That Latin phrase means something like "divine intervention," where an unexpected event or power solves a situation the heroes of the story can't. Many critics say that writers can't write a story like that!

Actually, you can. And I have, although I don't want to spoil the surprise by telling you which of my books include such events.

The twists and turns of history have inspired me to try to make my stories as unpredictable as life itself. However, I'll be the first to admit that I used to get so excited by what was happening (the plot) that I would forget to delve into the characters' feelings. As an avid reader, and writer, I've come to the conclusion that authors are usually either plot authors or character authors. Most people have a natural tendency toward one or the other, although the universe occasionally delivers a writer who has equally mastered both. For me, someone like J. K. Rowling fits this category. I just can't say which kind of author she is because of how well she straddles both.

There's a problem associated with being a plot author—sometimes the sheer enormity of your plots and subplots can become overwhelming. It may be nearly impossible to keep track of them all. One author lost me by the sixth book in his series because of this. I realized after reading an over-eight-hundred-page book that he'd taken all his plots ahead only twenty-four hours. We never circled back to some of the lines that especially interested me, so the end of the novel left me both frustrated and disappointed. I've experienced this as an author too—something similar happened with my novel *Landmoor*. The plot had overrun the story. I had lost sight of the purpose of what I was trying to do, which was to tell a story and make a reader feel.

It was my wife who finally pointed this out to me after reading some rough drafts of my earlier novels—even the post-*Landmoor* ones. It was difficult for her to keep track of all the twists and turns. What she really wanted was to delve more deeply into a couple of the characters. To understand how the events of the book affected them on an emotional level. Her favorite book of all time is *To Kill a Mockingbird*, and she used this novel to explain why it's so important to have one or two touchstone characters. Of course, *Mockingbird* also has a compelling plot. There's the story about Atticus Finch defending a black man accused of a heinous crime he didn't commit. Of course, there's also the bit about Boo Radley and the kids. At its heart, though, it's a story about childhood in the South. It's Scout's story. And sticking to her point of view enabled the author to explore everything about society that she wanted to explore and reveal. It followed the Han Solo principle, even though we only heard from Scout.

As someone who is, at heart, a plot author, I had no problem conjuring up stories, civilizations, governments, religions, and magic systems. Piece of cake. My Achilles heel was developing characters who'd feel as real to readers as Scout did to my wife.

To address this deficiency, I decided to try a new method of writing, with the help of a couple of old D&D friends. One of the classes I was taking in college at the time was on the history of cities, which I found fascinating. It inspired me to invent a fictional city called Minya. The city had different tiers belonging to the groups who lived in them. Rather than write the first book, *Tears of Minya*, in the usual manner, I asked my friends to help me by roleplaying the two main characters of the story. Becoming a character is one of the fun things about D&D, and it's natural for seasoned players to adopt the persona of the being they are playing. One of the characters in this series was Jaylin Warnock, a new recruit to the Espion in Minya. (Many of you will recognize that I recycled the term Espion in my Kingfountain Series to denote the king's force of spies.) The other was Gabe Finch, an executioner from the Tier of Aster, the religious quarter. I eventually added a third person, a mixed-blood scholar who came to lead the outcasts of the Tier of the Infidel. The brother of one of my friends was so intrigued by this strange form of storytelling that he wanted to be part of it, so I invented this character for him.

I would write a scene for each of my friends like pages from a novel. They could not read each other's portions. Each scene ended with a decision to be made by the character—a decision my friends would make as Jaylin or Gabe. (At this point, we lived in different cities, so we did all of this by email.) After they decided, I would integrate their answers into the next scene of the book, moving each of their stories forward based on the choices they'd made. Sometimes we'd have many back-and-forth interchanges in one day to provide the dialogue for a scene or discuss some critical choice Jaylin or Gabe had made.

I would write these little scene snippets during my lunch break at work or in the evenings after homework. And, if I'm being honest, sometimes during work time. Some people kill time at work browsing the internet or playing games or shopping on their phones. I wrote books. The self-justification didn't make it right, but I am being honest.

Talking with my friends about their motivation for the various decisions they made as Jaylin and Gabe helped me learn how to make characters more three-dimensional. This exercise allowed me to get into the skin of these characters and see the world through their eyes instead of those of the omniscient narrator residing in my brain. Often my friends would surprise me with their decisions, just as they used to in our old D&D adventures.

The experience of working on the Minya books taught me another truth. People like to be surprised and delighted. Neuroscientists, such as Dr. Gregory Berns, have done research on this, in fact, discovering that it lights up certain pleasure centers in the brain. Twists and surprises are a must. Readers are always trying to predict what is going to happen. If they get it wrong 100 percent of the time, they'll become bored or frustrated. If they guess it right 100 percent of the time, the same thing happens. There must be a balance between right guesses and wrong guesses to keep all those neurons firing in a happy way. This insight is the main reason why I have so many twists in my books and why I balance some that readers can figure out versus ones they can't.

This writing exercise worked so well that I ultimately wrote four books in the Minya series. These books, and the unique way I wrote them, helped stretch me in critical ways as a writer. While I don't have real people "playing" the characters in my novels now, I do try to make each one feel like a real person who makes believable choices. Which is not the same as saying they must always be logical. Trust me, I'm not logical all the time. No one is. By "believable" I mean that the characters choices must fit with the patterns we've established for them over time. Now, it's sometimes tempting to have a character act . . . well, completely out of character, to allow for a shocking twist. But that sort of thing can create a negative perception in our readers' minds. And that's not the kind of emotional response I'm seeking.

After finishing these Minya stories, I thought that I might have better luck selling them to a publisher instead of *Landmoor*, which I was still revising. I was also using my writing time on Saturdays to work on a series called the Kingmaker series, based on another set of D&D adventures that I'd done with my friend as one character and my wife as another. I had three different worlds that I was writing in at the time—Landmoor, Kingmaker, and Minya—and I figured one of them could possibly lead to my goal of getting a publishing contract. I still didn't know about the first million words principle. But I was applying it all the same.

Understanding the motivations of characters became part of the secret sauce. It made the writing more enjoyable. Deeper. When my wife read some of my new work, she would comment on the improvement of the emotional element of the storytelling. And usually add comments like "more like this" and "give me more" when I delved into my character's inner thoughts and feelings. No matter how much I included, it wasn't enough.

I also hit an interesting crossroads around this time. My plan had been to go to grad school and get my PhD to become a history professor. I finished my bachelor's degree in 1996, graduating at the top of my class. I'd applied to grad school at some prestigious universities in the country, notable for their history programs. None of them accepted me. I entered the master's program at the college I was going to and set a goal to finish my master's degree in one more year before trying again.

To save money, we moved in with my wife's parents while we both worked full-time, and I went to school mostly at night. I joined the Academic Senate that year as well as the Board of General Studies, hoping both would improve my chances of getting into Stanford, which was the university I dreamed of attending. Moving meant my wife and I no longer taught early morning seminary, but I was still getting up at five in the morning to balance all of my commitments to school, Intel, and church.

I had changed jobs within Intel by this point, no longer working for Intel U but for a group called Workforce Development, which partnered with local community colleges to improve the curriculum so that graduates understood the tech industry better and would be better-suited for jobs in our factories. I knew a lot about how academia worked, and it was a natural fit. The job was enjoyable enough that I began to wonder if going off to earn a PhD was really the right thing for me.

Just as I'd planned, I finished my master's degree in history in one year. Writing my thesis was one of the most mind-numbing writing assignments I'd ever had. It was pure torture to me. I loved doing research. That always lit up my brain and helped me improve my concentration skills. But writing academic papers stifled every creative neuron inside my brain because the language had to conform to the norms in academia.

After completing my master's, a decision had to be made. One of the universities I'd applied to, the University of

Colorado at Boulder, accepted me into their PhD program. I even had the chance to fly there to meet the faculty.

We'd reached the crossroads. Would we move to Boulder and continue to pursue the dream I'd worked on so hard for five years? Did I really want to pour myself into faculty panels, academic writing, and deep research as I'd done during the last year? I still loved teaching but knew the adage for university life—publish or perish.

Publishing novels wouldn't count.

IMPOSTER SYNDROME

In the final analysis, my wife and I decided not to go for the PhD program in Boulder, Colorado. In one respect, the decision had been creeping up on us for years. Life in academia wasn't what I'd hoped it would be. The prospect of spending four to six more years doing the same type of work just weighed on me, as did the notion of writing an academic paper that was several hundreds pages. It just wasn't the kind of writing I was interested in doing. While I liked the idea of being a history professor, I didn't want to put in the time to get there—or continue to put out academic papers once I did. Remember, you must want the consequences of what you want. I'd seen some of these consequences, and they made me rethink my previous plans.

We'd only just decided to stay when I learned my position with Workforce Development wouldn't become a full-time job—and, indeed, might be going away altogether. Thankfully, another position had opened up in Human Resources—a staffing consultant supporting the D2 factory. I threw my hat in the ring, hoping that I would have a chance since I understood a lot more about the factory after working in

Workforce Development. I got along really well with several of the shift managers. A strange thing happened during my interview, though. The two shift managers who interviewed me for the staffing consultant job asked how badly I really wanted it. They wanted to know whether I would consider working for them instead.

The opportunity came out of nowhere. I was open to the experience, so they offered me the opportunity to join D2 (Intel's research fab in Silicon Valley) as a night-shift supervisor. Talk about a twist of fate that I hadn't been considering or expecting. Because of my training in HR and experience in Workforce Development, they both thought I would make a good addition. I was assigned to work on shift 6, but my schedule was different from my peers because I was needed during the daytime as well. I ended up working a modified twelve p.m. to twelve a.m. shift.

Once I started in my new position, it felt as if I had traveled to a new planet.

My understanding of the factory and what went on inside was incredibly limited at the outset. I had to learn a whole new vocabulary, only some of which I'd picked up while working in HR, and I went through training courses, including the very HAZCOM class I used to supervise.

I'll tell you, this was when I first began to understand and experience imposter syndrome. It wasn't until a TED talk by Amy Cuddy called "Your Body Language May Shape Who You Are" that I had heard about that term, but I experienced it anyway. Imposter syndrome is a mental game we play with ourselves. It's that nagging inner critic I mentioned earlier, telling us that we don't belong, that we'll never belong. That we are not enough. This voice fills us with anxiety and internal pressure to succeed as well as the fear of being found out by others as an imposter.

The reason I started to feel it so strongly at the time was that many of the people I worked with had graduated from top-notch schools in the country (MIT, Stanford, Cal Poly). They were always quick to mention their credentials to one another. I noticed how some people treated others differently because of their education. We all wore blue Intel badges, but where you were *before* you got your badge seemed to matter. A degree was like a poker chip to be played, granting instant credibility and respect. And I quickly became ashamed that I'd graduated from the local school, with a degree in history no less. What was I doing working at an R&D fab? Some of my peers had gone to the same prestigious schools that had rejected me.

Around this time it struck me that my history degree wouldn't cut it long term. My managers had overlooked my lack of training because they'd gotten to know me on the job and thought I'd be a good fit. But I realized that if I intended to make Intel a career, I would need to get a degree that would better serve the company.

After five years of college, I felt burned out. I was still learning the ropes in my new job, and the last thing I wanted to do was go back to school. My wife recognized that I was procrastinating furthering my education, despite knowing what I needed to do, and we finally had a long heart-to-heart one time while visiting my parents' cabin in the mountains. The longer I delayed switching majors, she suggested, the harder it would get. I also remember asking my dad for advice. He has a PhD in electrical engineering and had worked at Hewlett-Packard for most of his career before joining a start-up. I knew I could only do school part-time while working full-time and was afraid it might take a couple of years to finish my new degree. I thought getting an MBA would be the most useful for me, as I didn't want to become an engineer. My dad listened and then asked me a question that really crushed the excuses I was inventing to delay the inevitable. He said he knew it might take two to three years to finish my MBA. How old would I be, in two to three years, without an MBA? His question made me smile. The time was going to pass anyway. I'd rather do the work now than wait until I was older and had even more responsibilities to juggle.

Procrastination is the default decision that most of us make. There's an excellent TED talk by Tim Urban called "Inside the Mind of a Master Procrastinator," where he shows a bubble chart of how many weeks we have in our lives. It's so easy to let the years slip through our fingers. I'm grateful I tackled my MBA then instead of waiting. It's paid off many times over.

Intel agreed to pay for my MBA, so long as I retained good grades. Once again, I was back at that same college doing classes one night a week and one Saturday a month.

I achieved some success working in TMG (the technology and manufacturing group). Being part of the hiring team gave me exposure to the factory and engineering management. I began to realize that even though I was not a graduate from a top-tier school, I was just as smart and capable as my peers. That experience really helped me turn down the volume on that voice in my head. In fact, being the new person allowed me to ask lots of "dumb questions." No one ever criticized me for asking them, and the more I asked, the more I learned. I think people in high-pressured environments try to pretend they already know what they're doing because they don't want to look dumb. But asking questions isn't a sign of stupidity. It shows you want to learn.

Imposter syndrome is a plague suffered by most writers. By this point on my writer's journey, I'd had one story published, but I believed that I wouldn't become a *real* writer until I got a book deal from a large publisher. There were people who paid to have their books published by someone else (called vanity presses). I had considered doing that, but the very word *vanity* triggered my imposter syndrome. I wanted to make it legitimately. People were impressed when I told them one of my hobbies was writing, but the conversation usually came around to whether or not I'd been published. Even today, people ask me why I don't have a movie deal, as if having a movie made of one of my books will prove I've finally arrived. The insidiousness of imposter syndrome is unrelenting. It can never be satisfied. Each time you meet a milestone, the marker of success gets moved farther away.

In order to tune down that voice, it's critically important to recognize the sources of imposter syndrome in your life. Sometimes your inner critic, as we've called it, sounds like your own voice—and so you assume it is. Sometimes the voice might sound like someone else, perhaps a parent or a sibling who's always said you'll never amount to anything.

Imposter syndrome itself has served as an inspiration to me. It's critical to the character development of Sera in my Harbinger Series, and readers of my Muirwood books will recognize this insidious voice as the whispers of the Myriad Ones.

But what is the source of imposter syndrome? Did we, as some neuroscientists may think, evolve to criticize ourselves and others?

People call this voice by different names. I mentioned earlier that Napoleon Hill called it the Devil, Steven Pressfield called it Resistance, and Brené Brown calls it shame.

I'm certain Napoleon Hill had it right. And he was too ashamed to call it out and publish his beliefs during his lifetime. His book *Outwitting the Devil* was published posthumously. In it, he describes his own depression as a dark cloud that hung over him and stymied him for months, making him feel like a failure. Ultimately, he came to the conclusion these feelings originated from a negative force in the universe—one intent on keeping us stuck in a rut. He feared he'd be mocked for exposing himself and describing *what we all feel every day*. Steven Pressfield was also hesitant to write about Resistance, which he eventually described as a force that attacks us whenever we try to pursue a higher purpose in life. And Brené talks about the debilitating voice of shame and how it propels us into a downward cycle that is hard to escape.

Did you know that the Hebrew word for Satan means "accuser" or "adversary"? That is the source of the inner critic that fuels imposter syndrome.

It takes a lot of effort to overcome the effects of the accuser. It takes near-constant effort. I heard the story of the first individuals who tried to reach the North Pole. What they didn't realize was that the ice shifted beneath them constantly, bringing them south every moment they stood still. They'd wake up the next morning and find they'd lost ground, even though they hadn't moved.

Whether or not you believe that there is an evil force influencing your mind doesn't limit its ability to influence your mind. Napoleon Hill skirted around this so much in his book *Think and Grow Rich*. He was quick to call the source of goodness God, or Infinite Intelligence. But he was embarrassed to talk about the other force that tries to insinuate itself into our minds through our own thoughts.

You will struggle to write your first million words or put in your ten thousand hours, however you want to measure your goal, if you don't first learn to recognize the two voices inside your head and how to tell them apart so that you know which to listen to and act on.

If you write a sentence and then have to stop because you feel compelled to edit it over and over until it is "passable," then guess what. You're listening to the wrong side. It's like trying to cross a field wearing ankle irons. You won't make it very far. By turning off that voice, you can write page after page without constantly worrying if it's garbage.

I've learned the words flow better and stronger when I ignore that voice in my head. I don't even let my internal editor have a say on my writing until a lot of time has passed to give me perspective. The only way I've been able to become as prolific as I am is by learning how to manage this voice so that I can get into a flow state and write the stories that are in my heart.

Imposter syndrome is real. Just remember that *you're* not the imposter. Whoever is trying to crush your spirit and prevent you from achieving your godly purpose in life . . . they are the imposter. It says in the scriptures that the devil—an angel fallen from heaven—transforms himself as an angel of light (2 Corinthians 11:14 and 2 Nephi 9:9). See? He's the chief imposter. He got kicked out. He's the reject. Not you.

And if you are going to achieve what you were sent to accomplish in this life, the purpose you were created for, then you'll have to learn to recognize and then shut that voice down. Especially when you believe it is your own mind talking to you or encouraging you to quit. It isn't.

Whatever your interpretation of this voice, know that it is not yours, and it is not right.

FAILURE

There is a saying that goes something like this: If you absolutely knew you would not fail, what would you dare to do?

But here is the reality. No matter how achievable (or unachievable) your goals, you will undoubtedly experience failure along the way. It is inevitable, like the tide, the rising of the sun, paying taxes—even death itself. In fact, I don't believe it's possible to achieve success without tasting failure before or after it. It gets you either way. Failure is one of the main ingredients of life. And I think it's here to test us in a specific way. You see, it tests our determination. Or resilience. It's the only way those things are strengthened. As I mentioned earlier, I make a habit of reading the biographies of famous people, and there's one common theme: failure.

Oh, but we *hate* failing! Here's the rub—you can't have success without it. You need to learn the lessons that each imparts, and typically the failure comes first. For some of us, the failure might be crushing enough that we decide to stop trying. But we can't skip it. In fact, it's often a signal we're on the right track.

Let me rephrase the statement I started with. If you absolutely knew that you would eventually succeed, what would you dare to do? All I did was add another adverb. "Eventually." If you knew it was a foregone conclusion that you would succeed in the end, wouldn't that motivate you to keep trying?

Let me tell you about some of my personal failures. They are painful to talk about, and at the time, they were excruciating. But I learned so much from those experiences, and they don't haunt me anymore. You see, in addition to resilience, determination, and perseverance, failure also can give you courage.

My dream of becoming an author didn't fade while I was working in D2. In fact, it only took me a year or so to realize that running a production line was not my calling in life. Although I'd learned a lot, my creativity muscle was begging for a way to be exercised. After working in one area of the factory for a year, my manager asked if I would be willing to join the main part of the factory and manage one of the more challenging functional areas—Implant. It was a sign of my managers' trust in me that they decided to put me there. It also meant higher exposure to challenges and problems.

I agreed to take the new job, feeling confident that I could handle it, even though I was learning that working in the fab wasn't very fulfilling. I thought I'd been a decent supervisor, and it was a new experience managing a different team. Working all night took a toll on me, especially while I was still trying to earn my MBA.

Soon after my transition, one of my Implant equipment technicians asked if he could switch to the day shift because a position had opened up. I counseled with Cliff about the decision before making it. He, too, was uncomfortable with it, but we felt we should let the employee go if he wanted to.

Little did I know the consequences that lay ahead of that decision. Nor did I foresee other changes that would come with the new year, 1999. My wife became pregnant, and the experience of parenthood was impending. I was nervous about what to expect.

This was the decade of the dot-com boom. New companies sprang up overnight, and it seemed as if the rules of business had changed forever. People invested money in the stock market directly, and my boss taught me how to day-trade. Everyone made money on internet stocks. There was no way to lose. Interestingly, even in my MBA classes, it felt as though the business textbooks were already becoming outdated. The world was being made anew.

Some of the tech stocks I bought went down, but experience taught me when to cut my losses and invest in higher-growth stocks. Mostly, if you just waited long enough, the stocks would eventually recover. It was a form of gambling, but I didn't realize it at the time. I was too caught up in the euphoria of the times and felt as if I could succeed at anything.

Around this time, I recall the leaders at a semiannual general conference of the church warning us to be prudent and wise with our money. The markets were unstable and could fall as well. I ignored this counsel, as well as the lessons I was learning in business school. Surely the old rules no longer applied. It felt as though we were at the dawn of a new era, riding a wave to prosperity. This was it!

After my wife and I found out she was pregnant, we used the Intel shares I'd earned as an employee and the savings we'd accrued from living with her parents to put a down payment on a house. After buying one, I still had some money left over, and I was also making money day-trading. Perhaps I could invest in my writing as well. I started wondering if I could turn my only published short story, "The Wishing Lantern," into a children's book. With the advent of Amazon, I realized there was a bookstore I could sell my creation in that spanned the entire country, soon . . . the world. I talked to two of my best friends, Jeremy and Brendon, about the idea. Jeremy was an English major and had experience in layout design and making websites. Brendon was an attorney. The more I researched the publishing industry, the more I suspected this trend toward technology would utterly transform it. Anyone could publish a book, including the three of us.

All I needed was an artist who could breathe life into the story with colorful illustrations.

It turned out that one of the shift supervisors I worked with at D2 had a brother who was a fantasy artist doing artwork for Magic: The Gathering. We conversed about the idea, and I researched offset-printing costs to establish a budget. It was exciting, thrilling even. I was about to see a dream fulfilled. With my wife's support, Jeremy, Brendon, and I created a publishing company called Amberlin Books. The word Amberlin comes from my Landmoor Series. In the language of the Shae, it means "bringer of light." Basically, my company was named after a word I'd invented while playing D&D. We set aside a budget to handle the artwork and print costs.

Randy Gallegos, the artist, brought the two main characters, Hickem Tod and Estellionata, to life. I can't describe how it felt to see the initial sketches bring something that had started in my imagination to life. It was a rush, and to this day it remains one of my favorite parts of the publishing process— although my other books have not been illustrated, I love seeing what concepts artists come up with for the covers of my books. We even had Randy do watercolor copies of the two main character sketches, Hickem Tod and Estellionata, to sell along with the first hundred copies. My first child was born in 1999, a daughter, and I dedicated the book to her. It was finally happening. I'd published my first book.

We waited in anticipation for the books to arrive from the printer. Most of them came to me, but some boxes were shipped to Jeremy's and Brendon's homes.

All of us emailed friends and family to see if they wanted to buy the books. We got over a hundred orders and set to work to fill them. That's when we noticed the first problem. As soon as we took the books out of the box, the covers began to warp. It happened with every single one. We couldn't ship the books like that, and with fear in my gut, I worried I'd been taken advantage of by the printer. I called them and explained the problem and sent in a few samples. They realized the problem was in the gluing of the cover, and they could treat it so that it wouldn't continue to happen. I had to ship all the boxes back to them, at my expense. But they fixed and returned them. And when I pulled a book out, it didn't warp.

We set to work sending out the purchased copies. I thought the book was so stunning visually that thousands would want a copy. But it didn't happen. Although it was listed on Amazon, most of our purchases came from family and friends. I had boxes and boxes of books in my garage and at my friends' houses.

It was easy to produce a book, I discovered, but selling it was much trickier. I even tried visiting some local bookstores to see if they would buy copies to sell in their stores. The experience was totally humiliating. I would see an awkward look drift across the manager's face as I tried to pitch my book. It was obvious they were wondering how to say no without hurting my feelings. After this happened a few times, I realized that I was not in the right line of business. I began to see why publishers hired a sales staff to do the pitching for them. I couldn't bypass the middleman as easily as I had thought. Yes, I could get my book listed online. But how would my target audience even know it was there?

As the months ticked by and the boxes of books sat unopened in my garage, I realized gradually the magnitude of the mistake I'd made. I'd promised my wife that the investment would be recouped easily. Indeed, I'd hoped the book would turn a tidy profit, which would fund Amberlin Books to publish my Landmoor Series next. It would become a virtuous cycle of success, and we'd eventually help publish other authors as well. But it wasn't going to happen yet. Having just bought a new house, we could have used that money to help put in a backyard. Instead, I was spraying weed killer on everything that grew back there.

Night-shift life also wasn't very conducive to raising babies. I wouldn't stay on night-shift hours during my days off as many did. I waffled back and forth, and each week I became more exhausted. Our daughter was also colicky, which made our first months of parenting miserable. I thought I'd know what to do as a parent because I came from a large family, but each child is different, and being an older sibling is very different from being a parent.

Something had to give.

My manager called me on one of my days off. He never did that. Something had gone seriously wrong, and the line was down. The problem was tracked back to one tool, which had been pulled for preventative maintenance during my last shift. It turned out a filter had been installed upside down. Instead of catching bad particles, it had been spraying them everywhere. The alarms on the tool had been bypassed to get it back in use more quickly. It wasn't until the chips started failing much farther down the line that the engineers began to realize there was a serious problem. Days had gone by, running bad product through that one enormous tool the size of a sports utility vehicle. It was a multimillion-dollar mistake, and it had happened on the shift I oversaw.

I wasn't the new kid anymore. I was at ground zero of a line-down situation.

Just as sharks are drawn to blood, so are engineers to factory supervisors who don't run their areas properly. I'd seen it happen to others, but now I was experiencing it firsthand. The most senior equipment tech who'd overseen the maintenance was called in as well. And that's when things became tricky. Yes, it was technically his fault. He'd put the filter in wrong.

But the shortcuts he'd used to disable the alarms and get the tool back up to production were tricks of the trade he'd learned from other employees. When this came to light, it didn't just make our shift look bad, it made the entire functional area look bad. If we fired the tech for negligence when everyone else did the same thing, it could lead to a wrongful termination lawsuit. It was a mess of gargantuan proportions. It would have been really easy sacrificing my senior equipment tech on the altar. But I didn't feel it was the right thing to do, especially since he'd learned the bad habits from some of the engineers and peers he worked with.

The outcome of the investigation hit us all hard. I had to formally reprimand my technician, and everyone had to endure weeks of additional training to ensure this sort of thing didn't happen again.

When it came time for midyear performance reviews, I was given a substandard review, labeled a "slower" (which meant I was trending *slower* than my peers, which put me at risk for formal discipline at the next full review cycle and could lead to termination). I'd seen it happen to others before. No one ever wanted to get a slower. Now it had happened to me. I'd hoped to continue my career at Intel until I got published. Now, my job was on the line. Had I made a mistake by switching majors? Should I have gone to the PhD program in Boulder, Colorado, after all?

Then, since trouble often comes in threes, the stock market bubble burst.

I'd invested most of our savings in the stock market, and we'd also leveraged my Intel stock. I felt like a fool. One internet stock that I'd purchased, PSI Net, literally fell to zero.

The shares became *worthless* as the company went bankrupt. I was one of many fools left holding the bag at the end, just as my MBA classes had taught me could happen, but I had been too blind to see because everyone had been doing the same thing.

Sometimes when I look back, I can't believe I survived everything that hit me at once. I'd never experienced situational depression until that time in my life. Colicky baby. MBA program. Black sheep Implant supervisor. Savings liquidating almost overnight. My first book failing.

My mind was mired in the *woulda-coulda-shoulda*s, and imposter syndrome hit hard. Why had I chosen to take the more challenging job at work? If I hadn't, another supervisor would have taken the blame for the line problem. Why had I thought that I could start my own publishing company? What did I know about *selling* books?

I looked for opportunities wherever I could to get rid of inventory from those boxes of books still sitting in my garage. Near the end of the year, there was an Intel craft fair where I'd requested table space—on my day off—to sell copies of *The Wishing Lantern* to other employees. I actually sold quite a few that day and had fun signing the books. But again, it felt as if I was an imposter, someone pretending to be an author.

In a strange twist of fate, which isn't all that strange if you recognize there's a higher power watching over us, someone approached the table whom I recognized. It was a girl I knew from high school. In fact, it was the girl I'd sat by during math class who had seen me editing a manuscript and asked to read it. She remembered me, and of course, I'd never forgotten her and her kindness and encouragement. I asked what she was doing at Intel of all places. She was a temp there. I told her that's how I had started as well. It gave me the chance to tell her that her encouragement, back in high school, had meant a lot to me and had led to me publishing the book. I offered to give her a copy of the book, but she insisted on paying for two—one for her and one for her niece.

It felt an awful lot like a sign that I should push through the mire and keep going.

I don't like the taste of failure. It's bitter. It's pungent. But pain is our best teacher. One of my favorite stories about failure is in Dale Carnegie's book *How to Win Friends & Influence People*. He tells the story of a mechanic who nearly killed a test pilot by doing a maintenance procedure wrong. The pilot miraculously survived and asked to see the mechanic who had worked on his plane and caused the engine to fail. The mechanic was miserable, but the pilot put his arm around the fellow and said he wanted him to work on his plane before his next flight. He knew that the mechanic would be more careful than anyone else, that he'd never make such a mistake again. I love that story. But that kind of attitude is rare, unfortunately. And I say unfortunately because it should happen more than it does. We expect perfection from imperfect people.

We all fail at things. How we are treated afterward—by others and, even more importantly, ourselves—either makes us want to do better, to be better, or it deflates and discourages us.

You are going to fail. I guarantee it 100 percent. But what I told you, that success comes down the road later? What if I guaranteed that? Would you still try? Would you take the risk?

That was a pretty dark year for me, but one thing was for certain.

Quitting just wasn't an option. Failure isn't falling down. Failure is *staying* down.

"No man can purchase his virtue too dear, for it is the only thing whose value must ever increase with the price it has cost us. Our integrity is never worth so much as when we have parted with our all to keep it."

—Ovid, Roman philosopher

INTEGRITY

In the end, failure really just means that your plans weren't good enough. It means you need to think your way out of a problem and create a better plan. Sometimes that one might fail too. And the next one. But each failure leads you to your next idea.

I'd learned a lot of lessons during that awful time. I'd learned that following the stock market crowd who believed basic principles of business didn't apply was wrong. It took losing most of our savings to learn this lesson. I'd learned that self-publishing a children's book was easy and that finding its audience was hard. I hadn't thought that out enough. I learned that parenting is hard and involves sleepless nights and stress, but that serving a helpless infant who cannot meet their own needs develops love. Seeing my baby girl smile at me and coo when I held her made the screaming sessions worth it. And I also learned that working in the factory wasn't the job for me. The next career I'd tried out had failed as well, but I realized that running production didn't match my skill sets either. This was good to know. I didn't like that I'd failed at all of these things. But I'd learned some important lessons.

The next lesson I learned turned out to be a pivotal moment.

I had been at Intel for seven years by this point and knew I was in trouble. I saw the writing on the wall. Have you ever wondered where that saying comes from? It's from the Old Testament, Daniel, chapter 5. The story takes place after the Israelites have been carried away into Babylon. All the sacred vessels, which had been taken from the temple of Jerusalem, were being used as party dishes in the king's court. The king, while making a feast of celebration, sees a disembodied hand writing on the wall. Daniel, the wisest counselor in Babylon, who has a prophetic gift for interpreting dreams, says that the writing predicts the downfall of the king. It's a story about pride. It's also a story that tells us God sees our actions, and we reap what we sow.

Since I'd been given that *slower* message at midyear, I knew better than to expect good news when our annual reviews were done in April. My manager had advised me to find another job within Intel before that happened. If I waited, I might not be able to transfer at all because poor performers weren't given the chance.

As I pondered my career choices and the fact that I was still working on my MBA, I thought about my experience in Workforce Development and how much I'd enjoyed that job. In working on partnerships with colleges, I had met people who had worked for Intel's Public Affairs group. They participated with news agencies, charities, and other public-facing opportunities. It seemed like the kind of organization that might be a good fit for me. I looked at Intel's job postings online and found two open positions in that group. I applied to both of them, along with a position in a group called TMG Sourcing. They were basically Intel's headhunters, recruiters who went to job fairs looking for possible candidates to hire.

The TMG Sourcing group contacted me almost immediately and began a round of interviews. It would be working in Human Resources again, and I not only had previous experience from my days at Intel U and Workforce Development, but I had firsthand experience in the fab and knew what the jobs were like. Being a recruiter would mean cold-calling candidates to try and persuade them to join Intel, which did not sound very appealing to me. I really wanted one of the Public Affairs positions, but I hadn't heard back from them yet, only that they were still gathering a candidate pool and that they'd contact me if they were interested.

During this period of high anxiety, I worried a lot. I had a difficult time controlling my thoughts as I ruminated on future outcomes. The night-shift schedule was incredibly difficult, and I found myself tortured by anxiety before starting my shift each week, afraid of what disaster might unfold next. My shift was still the proverbial black sheep of the factory family, and I felt the negative energy every time I went to work.

TMG Sourcing offered me the job. In my heart, I still wanted to work for Public Affairs, but I had an offer in hand and still hadn't even heard back from the hiring manager in the other group. Should I take the job I was offered or see if I could delay a decision?

Because I worked in the factory, my cubicle was located in the Robert Noyce Building, which was Intel headquarters in

Santa Clara. The job I wanted was on one of the upper floors, and we weren't exactly allowed to wander those floors during the night shift. In my state of mental agitation, I decided to take a walk by the hiring manager's desk. As I did so, I felt as if what I was doing was wrong. But I justified it to myself that I was a supervisor and could wander through the building if I wanted to. I stopped by the Public Affairs area and poked my head into the hiring manager's office. Then I left.

A while later, I came back, driven by a need to know if I even stood a chance at getting a job in that group. Again, I was overcome with the feeling that I shouldn't be there. I ignored the sensation and riffled through some of the papers on the hiring manager's desk, looking for some bit of evidence that they were trying to interview candidates. If I knew I wasn't on a shortlist, then I could abandon my hope that I'd get to work there. I knew I was prying, that I was doing something unethical, but again I justified it in my mind that it was night shift, no one would come, and what I was doing wasn't so bad.

I left and went back to my own desk, frustrated that I hadn't found anything and also relieved that I hadn't been caught and nothing bad had happened to me because of my night wanderings. I got a nudge from TMG Sourcing about the job offer and told them that I had also applied to another job and was waiting to hear back from them. I was given a window of time to make the decision, so I couldn't string it out for much longer.

The next night when I came to work, there were no messages from Public Affairs. I still had no idea whether I was even being considered as a candidate. I think I even sent the hiring manager an email asking about the timetable for their decision and heard back that it might be a few more weeks. Joseph Smith once said "there is no pain so awful as that of suspense." It's one of my all-time favorite quotes and a pillar of my writing. And I've felt it myself many times. Not knowing the outcome was torture. Should I accept the TMG Sourcing offer? Or should I hold out for something I thought was better?

The next night, I walked upstairs again, downplaying the warning in my mind for the third time because nothing had happened on my other visits. I went back to the hiring manager's office and sat in her chair. I looked again for evidence that she was starting on the hiring process. I found nothing and soon became quite comfortable in the chair and imagined what it would be like to work on that floor for their group. I wanted it so badly. I really didn't want to cold-call candidates and try to sell them on taking a new job.

Then I heard footsteps coming down the hall. I sat upright in the chair, a spasm of panic surging through me. My immediate reaction was that it was someone from Security. Maybe they had watched me on the surveillance cameras and were checking on me to find out what I was doing. My mind became a little frantic as I tried to come up with a reasonable sort of excuse.

You can imagine my surprise when the person coming down the hall wasn't Security. It was the hiring manager in Public Affairs. And I was sitting in her cubicle, in her *chair*. I knew what she looked like and couldn't imagine what terrible luck had coordinated such a meeting between us at long last. I'm sure you (reading this) also saw the "writing on the wall" before it happened. In my pride and conceit, I'd been blind to it. She had come to work at 3:30 in the morning. And she found me in her chair. Of course she wanted to know who I was and what I was doing there.

I stammered, I apologized, I blushed six shades of scarlet in absolute mortification. She couldn't make any sense out of my answers. I hardly could either. Through my fumbling words, I explained I had applied for a couple of openings in Public Affairs. But why would I be in her office in the middle of the night? Was I writing her a note? There was no evidence of that. My brain began to shut down as I lobbed a pathetic excuse to her that I was just trying to envision what it would feel like to work in her group. I apologized profusely, and she sent me away with an annoyed and suspicious look.

As I slunk back to my own cubicle again, I'd never felt such a deep sense of humiliation. I'd completely blown any chance of getting the job. Oh, she might remember me—but only as the creepy guy she'd found squatting in her cubicle in the middle of the night. When I got home after my shift, I told my wife what had happened, weeping in shame and regret. I'd made a huge mistake. And there was no denying that I'd felt a warning—more than one—about what I was doing.

That's why the quote from Ovid, before this chapter, has meant so much to me.

"No man can purchase his virtue too dear, for it is the only thing whose value must ever increase with the price it has cost us. Our integrity is never worth so much as when we have parted with our all to keep it."

It felt as if I had squandered mine. My desperation to find a better position had clouded my judgment. I had failed in every imaginable way, but the most painful failure was treating my integrity lightly because I thought no one was watching.

Our conscience can really scorch our hearts when we don't live up to our own values.

I realized that the hiring manager could report me to Security. That they could start an investigation against me. I prayed she wouldn't. If I remember it correctly, I might have even written her an apology.

I was a humbled man when I contacted TMG Sourcing and gratefully accepted their job offer. Although it paid 25 percent less and my commute time would double, the hours were normal, and they would continue to cover my MBA costs because Intel had already made the commitment. I hadn't lost the things that were most important to me. I was still a dad. And, in my heart of hearts, I was still a writer.

Having learned the importance of integrity the hard way, I value it all the more. This is why I write characters like Ankarette, Fitzroy, Lia, and others who hold tight to their principles regardless of the challenges life presents to them. When we find examples of integrity in the real world, we can't help but feel admiration. Emulation.

Looking back, I'm glad the hiring manager found me that night. It was excruciating, yes, but it was a life-changing moment for me. I became determined to work hard and overcome my failures. More importantly, I promised my wife and God that I would treat my integrity as a prized possession in the future. It put some steel into my spine, which I'd sadly been lacking up until that point. I've read in biographies of many famous people, notably Steve Jobs, that they felt the rules for normal people didn't apply to them. I think I had some of that arrogance. I think we all do.

Having integrity means doing the right thing, even if no one is watching. Because the truth is someone is *always* watching. No act of kindness goes unseen. No act of sin either. I've never seen the literal fingers of God writing on a wall. But I've seen plenty of evidence of it in my life. I get to choose what kinds of portents He writes.

My failures in 1999 and the beginning of 2000 brought me face-to-face with myself, and I found that I didn't respect myself very much. I decided a new year would bring a new start. That's the glorious thing about guilt. We can use it to beat ourselves up, which does no one any good, or we can use it to change. To alter course. To repent.

Russell M. Nelson taught that the word *repentance*, in its New Testament form, is the Greek word *metanoeo*. It means "to change" our mind, knowledge, spirit, and even our very breath.

Change always happens. And it's not always so bad. Change is the arc of character development, not just in books but in our own lives. When I write my stories, I don't start with perfect characters in perfect situations. That wouldn't feel real or interesting. The characters I create have to make important choices, as we all do, and sometimes those choices cost them.

Life is one of our best teachers.

JOHARI WINDOW

Our knowledge of other people is imperfect, and so is our knowledge of ourselves. Although we're all aware we have certain weaknesses and predelictions, each of us has a unique set of blind spots—aspects of our character or personality that are obvious to others but not to us. What interests me is another dynamic—the possibility that we may have hidden aspects of our character (weaknesses or talents) that no one is aware of, including ourselves. Those are the great unknowns. Welcome to an idea called the Johari window, a concept created by psychologists Joseph Luft and Harrington Ingham decades ago.

Johari Window

	Known to Self	Not Known to Self
Known to Others	Arena	Blind Spot
Not Known to Others	Façade	Unknown

While I learned this concept in a training class I took at Intel, it has played a role in how I develop characters in my novels. But let's discuss the concept a little more before we move on to the applications.

It's possible to work on our secret weaknesses because at least we know about them. One of mine is raw cookie dough. My favorites are chocolate chip and snickerdoodle dough, though I have several other favorites and most include brown sugar. I love brown sugar so much that when I was a kid, I snuck an entire box into the backyard with a spoon and started eating it all by myself. I thought I was especially clever for hiding the spoon in the box and leaving it under the hedge in the backyard so I could come back the next day to finish it off. When I arrived, it was waiting for me, and I quickly spooned a large portion into my mouth. Odd . . . there was a strange crunchy sensation. I took another spoonful. Crunch, crunch. Then, wincing with horror, I looked inside the box and saw squirming earwigs amid my golden, delicious treasure. I'm not sure how many I'd eaten in those mouthfuls, but not even that horrific experience ruined the taste for me.

One personal weakness I needed someone to point out to me is my tendency for sarcastic comments. My daughter recently bought a T-shirt that says "National Sarcastic Society—like we need your support." I love it. I've always been pretty good at zingers. But my wife pointed out to me that my zingers could really hurt, especially when I used them against my children. I didn't see it as a problem, really. Sarcasm is just a form of humor. But it was a blind spot for me. After she pointed it out and said that it might hurt my relationship with my kids, I realized she was right. Words do hurt—the more pointed they are, the more painful they can be. And so, with her loving suggestion, I began learning to control my tongue. It took someone else's eyes to see that particular weakness. The traits that we have—both the positive and negative ones—apply to the Johari window and to characters we write about. How well do we act on them when we are aware of them?

The personal weaknesses we know about aren't really a problem. We can make adjustments over time and try to do a little better every day. And if we, or those around us, recognize our talents, we are better able to develop them. But what about the unknowns—the hidden traits no one notices? How do you work on something like that?

Well, it takes some humility. Because we can always turn to someone who knows us better than we know ourselves. And if we ask, our friend will clue us in on some of these missing pieces. I'm talking about our connection with God. Let me share a quick example from my life.

I took piano lessons as a kid but quit when I was thirteen because my piano teacher thought my parents were wasting their money. But I actually took more of an interest in piano after the lessons stopped. I practiced when I wanted to and learned the songs I liked. Music was another outlet for creativity.

During high school, I even composed a few original pieces. It brought me joy, and I still like playing piano today. While my wife and I were living in our first home with our little daughter, the phone rang one Sunday afternoon. It was a church leader calling to ask if I would be willing to lead a choir composed of multiple congregations to prepare for a pageant at the Oakland Temple. I was shocked nearly speechless. As a young man, I had learned how to lead music (as in counting the beats per measure) and did it occasionally at church. But leading a choir? I'd never done anything like that before. I had no idea how to do it.

I asked the leader if he'd called the right person and explained my complete lack of experience and qualifications. Surely there was someone else who was far more suited for it. He listened to me and said he hadn't known and would get back to me. I felt relieved—sort of. Not long after, he called back and said that the leaders had discussed it, and they felt it was what God wanted me to do.

It was certainly outside my wheelhouse and definitely far beyond the outer borders of my comfort zone. But I said yes anyway. They assigned me a skilled pianist who would at least be able to play the music. I had only gone to the pageant once or twice in the past and didn't even know the pieces.

It turned out to be a totally awesome experience. Before that assignment was finished, my bishop called me to be the choir director for our local congregation. I had *two* choirs to lead for a while. What I didn't realize at the time was that I had a talent for it. A totally unforeseen (by me) talent. I loved that experience and really enjoyed the members of the choir who came to our house each week to practice. I've participated in choirs ever since.

The best way to learn about the unknown areas is to pray about them and seek answers, as well as to embrace opportunities that appear out of the blue. Often we say no because it's uncomfortable. I'm grateful that I didn't say no. That I had cultivated a pattern of saying yes to opportunities and trusted that, whatever happened, I'd learn something from the experience.

When new opportunities come your way, don't reflexively shun them. One just may reveal part of you to yourself that you didn't even know existed. It wasn't until I became a choir director that I learned how to finally hear the tenor line and, eventually, sing it. Not only did the experience give me a new appreciation for music and a new skill, it stretched my abilities and enabled new growth.

Most of the time, the areas I need to work on are my blind spots. I'm grateful to have a wife who helps me see those areas. They're not easy to hear. But if we're vulnerable enough, we can listen, and we will find that great new opportunities open before our eyes.

All of this applies to the characters I write about. When I create someone, I think about what they see about themselves and what they do not. Sometimes I attempt to make a character's blind spots visible to the reader. Take Maia, for example, from the Covenant of Muirwood Trilogy. Many readers have criticized her for being too forgiving of her flawed father. To me, this blind spot makes her feel more real. She can't see what's so obvious to us because she's in a horrible situation—one in which her instinctive loyalty to her father is in conflict with her loyalty to right and wrong. If you understand what drives your characters, they will feel more real, and there's a reason for that—our traits and our motivations are all part of the bedrock of who we are. They help determine how we develop as people.

SEEING WITH NEW EYES

In 1 Corinthians, Paul says that we "see through a glass darkly." A glass back then was a mirror, a smudged mirror in which we can't see ourselves very clearly. Then he continues and says, "but then face to face." Like the Johari window from the last chapter, we don't see ourselves very objectively at times. Sometimes we need another way of seeing ourselves with fresh eyes.

After my failure to recoup the costs of publishing my children's book *The Wishing Lantern*, my friends and I realized we needed a better plan. For many years, one of these friends, Brendon, had suggested creating a fantasy/science-fiction magazine. We even dreamed of selling it to Del Rey, our favorite publisher. With the birth of the internet, we realized we could build a website that would be available all over the world. Electronic magazines—or e-zines—were becoming popular. Magazines could be produced and distributed at a fraction of the cost.

I was still working on my MBA at this time and had started my new job as a recruiter for Intel in Santa Clara. I had a three-hour daily commute, but most days I took a train and then a bus to the Intel campus, which gave me time to do other things on the journey. On the days I had night classes, I would drive in.

I continued to spend a lot of time studying the publishing industry and how electronic distribution was changing the business model. In the past, a publisher had to print thousands of copies of a book to achieve a lower cost. There were shipping fees, warehousing fees, and ultimately destruction fees if the books didn't sell. All of these costs ate into the industry's profits. New technologies, like print-on-demand, meant that books could be printed when ordered, which decreased the need for large print runs, storage, and transportation. The first e-readers were still in development inside companies like Sony and Amazon and wouldn't be launched for several years.

We recognized that if we wanted to become a publisher, we needed loyal customers. We needed to offer more than just one children's book. We needed products to sell. Producing an e-zine would help develop a customer list, which would hopefully grow and allow us to offer them new products and publications. In 2001, the three of us brainstormed ideas for putting this together. We called it *Deep Magic* and decided to publish fantasy and science fiction that was more family friendly. The novel *Game of Thrones* had come out in 1997, ushering in an era of grimdark fantasy. More and more novels had antiheroes. We felt there was an untapped market for readers who didn't want all the sex, swearing, and gore.

In our very first issue, our introduction read as follows:

Note From the Editors

June 2002

Welcome to the first issue of **DEEP MAGIC**.

On our website, we use a tag-line: Safe places for minds to wander. Rather than bore you with a definition, we will try to explain it this way. If you walked into Disneyland, you would not see a lot of soda cans or ice-cream sandwich wrappers on the streets. If you opened a book by C.S. Lewis, you would not find any profanity. If you pop in the DVD of Shrek, however, you would find an ogre farting in a pond and killing fish. Welcome again to DEEP MAGIC – a clean (but sometimes irreverent) e-zine.

There seems to be a trend in the fantasy genre these days: "grit is in." Grab the latest George R.R. Martin novel if you'd like to read a great author describe incest, a lawless world that makes the 12th century seem like Boy Scout camp, and hopeless, heartbreaking situations where you secretly wish the protagonists will die to end their suffering. There is undeniably a market for this kind of fiction. But this e-zine is not oriented toward that market.

We had the skills among the three of us to create *Deep Magic*. Jeremy, who became the chief editor, knew the software required to publish digitally, plus he was an English major. Brendon handled contracts, and I did the marketing and outreach. It would be a free e-zine because we had a very small budget. We wouldn't pay for the stories, but the authors would at least have a publishing credit. Our hope was that the e-zine would draw attention to our publishing company.

Because I had changed jobs and left the factory in Santa Clara, I'd lost a big percentage of my pay. I worked hard and had a great manager who taught me some valuable skills, especially cold-calling strangers. That was uncomfortable, but sometimes it's a good thing to be propelled out of one's comfort zone. It's how we grow.

But after the dot-com bust, recruiters weren't needed as much anymore, so the head of staffing authorized the launch of Staffing Market Intelligence, a new organization designed to research global labor markets. They put some of their best recruiters, including me, into that team to kick-start it.

I wanted to get out of the Bay Area—the rough commute and high cost of living had become harder and harder to endure. I asked if I could relocate to another site, and my new manager said it didn't matter which one I chose.

We made the decision to find a more affordable place in Sacramento and sold our house on September 8, 2001. Well, that's the day we agreed on the price with the buyer, a family we knew who had been looking for a new home. The next week, as I was riding the train to work on Tuesday and trying to get some homework done, my wife began to page me about the terrorist attacks that had just happened in New York and DC.

Sometimes it takes a tragedy to see the world with different eyes. It was the most bipartisan time I could remember in my life. Congress sang "God Bless America" on the steps of the Capitol building. Our little girl kept noticing and talking about all the American flags that sprang up everywhere.

We'd spent weekends house-hunting in Sacramento. We found a neighborhood under construction in the Sacramento area that we really liked, but they wouldn't have homes available for months. We worried we'd be living with my in-laws for a year by the time a new house could be built. But because of 9/11, one of the buyers in that subdivision backed out of their home. We were the first on the waiting list. They offered it to us if we could move in by the end of the year, and we said yes. We drove there to sign the papers, only to discover the original owners had decided not to leave after all. Our real estate agent apologized and said that we weren't getting that house. Something about it felt wrong—it had felt like ours—but we were strangely peaceful about it. Things would work out. We trusted that God had a plan for our little family.

We went back home. About two weeks later, the developer called again. The people had backed out again, this time for good. They apologized for putting us through the ordeal, and we moved into our new house two days after Christmas.

It was because of 9/11 that we didn't launch *Deep Magic* in 2001. We felt it just wasn't the right time to kick off such a venture. I was in a new job in a group that I loved, my commute had shrunk by half, and we had a new house we loved and a swimming pool to help endure the hot, hot summers.

The next year, we built a new website, and I started recruiting authors to submit stories from online writing workshops. Life can surprise you. My experience as a cold-caller, which I'd hated in the beginning, had prepared me for reaching out and offering opportunities to total strangers. We found fantasy artists who would let us use their artwork for *free* in exchange for using banner graphics that linked to their websites and helped build traffic. We got an early boost from Charles Coleman Finlay, who sent an announcement about *Deep Magic* to a distribution list he was in charge of. The submissions began pouring in faster and faster.

Reading all those submissions began to open my eyes. I'd always seen the publishing world through the eyes of an author. Now I began to see it through the eyes of an editor. It was another *unknown* box in my personal Johari window.

Deep Magic never became the success we'd hoped it would be. But it helped me form a better understanding of the publishing process and become a better writer.

We had a group of volunteers who helped weed through the slush pile looking for good stories, but we all dedicated our time to reviewing submissions. Without paying for stories, we knew we wouldn't attract the best talent. So much of what I saw felt like copycats of other works. The tone, the voice, the characters—all felt like something I'd read before in the other stories submitted. The repeated clichés were endless. Then, once in a while, we'd stumble onto something different. Unique. A new voice. A new feeling.

That's what I realized editors were looking for. Not a rehashing of *Lord of the Rings* or the Shannara world. It's why *Game of Thrones* became popular so quickly. It was something *new*. Different. It flipped a trope on its head.

It's amazing what you can see when you have new eyes.

The insights didn't come all at once. It came story after story, submission after submission, contract after contract. Experience. Repetition. Concentration. Commitment. We had a monthly publishing cadence to hit, which added deadline pressure. Our team began to grow with volunteers. One of them, Usman Malik, a fantasy/horror writer from Pakistan, is still a friend today.

Then I got a new idea. What if I could use *Deep Magic* to talk to and learn from the authors I admired? I was hungry for their wisdom, and I suspected the same was true of our authors and readers.

SHOULDERS OF GIANTS

As I mentioned in the chapter "Crusts and Loaves," there's a quote from Bernard de Chartres that we are dwarves standing on the shoulders of giants. When you aspire to do something, you're drawn to study those who've already found success. I'd learned as much as I could about Terry Brooks's publishing journey since he was the one who first inspired me to write.

I've studied many authors' journeys over the years, and while they're all different, there are certain common themes. With the creation of *Deep Magic*, I was determined to do what I would have been too embarrassed to attempt otherwise. It gave me a platform to ask the questions I'd always wanted to ask of traditionally published authors. I was also humbled that so many responded positively and agreed to be interviewed or even to contribute a writing-craft article for *Deep Magic*.

Amazingly, the first author who responded to my request was Robin Hobb. I thought it was a long shot, but she was so nice and willing to help out. I got permission to recycle an article she'd previously written called "Fantasy and Clichés," in which she argued that using some clichés was a good thing. She also answered the two questions I'd decided to ask the authors who agreed to be featured in the e-zine. The first question was: How has the internet affected your relationship with readers and/or publishers? (We were an e-zine after all, and I wanted to understand how the industry was changing the publishing world. Why not find out firsthand what was going on from people on the inside?) The second question I asked was: Tell us the story of how your first book was published.

Both questions were designed to be open-ended so the author could elaborate as much or as little as they wanted. When I got Robin's responses, which are published in the June 2002 issue of *Deep Magic* on Scribd, both answers gave me insights that I wouldn't have come up with on my own. Her answer to the first question focused on the changing relationship between readers and writers. In the past, the only real way of connecting with a favorite author was either coming to an event the author was at like a convention or book signing, or writing them a letter and mailing it to their publisher. If you were lucky, you'd hear back months later. When I think about all the ways that readers and writers interact *now*, via Facebook, Twitter, Instagram, Reddit, it's a totally different world. There are ample opportunities for real-time interactions, and publishers and readers expect authors to be so much more available and responsive than they were in the past.

The second insight I got from Robin's interview was the serendipity of her discovery, which is similar to many authors I know.

Robin had written a short story for an anthology, and the anthology went on to win the World Fantasy Award that year. She had included as a preface to her story that it was part of a larger project she'd been working on. And she had been, at the time. But had stopped a year or so later when she moved to Seattle. Once there, she contacted the editor of the anthology, who mentioned that an editor at Ace had liked Robin's story and wondered if anything had come of the project. That positive feedback spurred Robin to reach out to the Ace editor, and she ultimately signed a multibook deal with them.

Robin's takeaway from the experience was that writing wasn't enough. She should have started submitting earlier.

That wasn't *my* takeaway, though. In almost every story I heard from authors, there was this miraculous serendipity that played a large part in their discovery. A chain of events connecting people at the right time in the right place. It had happened with Terry Brooks. It had happened with J. K. Rowling. And ultimately, it happened for me too.

Overnight success doesn't come overnight. There is a cosmic timetable at work in our lives, one we cannot and should not see. I see this as divine intervention, not serendipity. Why did Robin feel the need to reach out to that anthology editor when she did? Was it a hunch, a feeling?

Whatever you wish to call them, we need to pay attention to those little nudges that happen in our lives. We can't make them happen. We don't know when they will happen. But we must be prepared to respond to them when they do. We can do this by writing our first million words. By failing and getting up again. By continuing to try, no matter what setbacks push us off track.

During those first years of *Deep Magic*, we were able to interview or get writing-craft articles from Terry Brooks, Brandon Sanderson, George R. R. Martin, Robert Jordan, and many, many others. They were all willing, especially if we respected their time and kept it short and simple. After the movie *Pirates of the Caribbean* came out, I even sought out Jay Wolpert, who wrote the original screenplay. He wasn't interested in answering an email. He insisted I call him at home and ask him the questions and write up the interview myself. I learned some amazing things from him, little details that actually ended up in subsequent movies.

One of my favorite experiences, however, happened in New York City. I flew there on a business trip for Intel—I'd been invited to attend and present at a labor economics conference at Columbia University. It was the first time I got to visit Manhattan. I was able to meet a mentor of mine at the conference, Michael Teitelbaum from the Sloan Foundation (astute readers will recognize the names Sloan and Teitelbaum from my Harbinger Series).

When some people visit New York City, they want to see the Statue of Liberty, Time Square, or Central Park. I wanted to see Random House. I told a contact I'd made at Bantam Dell, which is part of Random House, that I'd be in New York City soon and asked to interview her in person. My contact, Betsy Hulsebosch, was the head of marketing at the time, and she graciously agreed. I arrived as scheduled, a day before the conference, and took a taxi to the Random House building. Betsy was very welcoming and kind, and I also got to meet Anne Groell. She invited me into her office to chat, which was pretty amazing, and took a phone call from George R. R. Martin about a delay in his next book while I was there. She then offered to let me take any books I wanted off the bookshelf, most of which were books they had published (some of them early copies). I was like a kid with a box of brown sugar—without the earwigs. I took many and thanked Anne for the opportunity to meet her team. Anne also put me in touch with many of the authors they worked with for future interviews.

Prior to the trip, I had started publishing my novel *Landmoor* in *Deep Magic* in serialized form in the hopes that I'd develop a following. Remember, one of the specific reasons we'd started the e-zine was to build an audience for our publishing company (or attract the notice of another publishing house). Either way, my thinking was like *Field of Dreams*. If I build a readership, opportunities would come.

After going to New York and meeting folks at Random House, I felt confident that I'd be able to secure a book deal. I'd learned quite a bit about the publishing world in my research for *Deep Magic*. I secretly hoped that Anne would ask to see some of my writing. But that didn't happen. Months went by, and each month we published a new issue. Our readership continued to grow. I'd already been writing the sequel to *Landmoor* as well as other books and decided to include them in *Deep Magic* too. Charles Dickens had made his name selling serialized novels to newspapers. I figured I stood a chance at building a fan base the same way. In May 2003 we published *Landmoor* as the next offering from Amberlin Books, almost one year after launching the e-zine.

Sales were a total flop.

Thankfully, it wasn't the financial setback I'd experienced previously since we used print-on-demand instead of the regular offset printing. Many of the readers of the e-zine bought copies of the novel, but just a small fraction of the total readership. We couldn't understand why.

I realized I'd made another blunder. We hadn't only given away sections of the book for free—we'd given away the whole thing. The audience didn't want to pay for something they'd already gotten for free. We decided that instead of giving away all of the book in *Deep Magic*, we'd provide samples only. We went to work preparing *Silverkin* for publication and thought we'd learned our lesson.

It was around this time that I received a sign. A nudge if you will. It came in the form of a promotional flyer from the Book Passage, a bookstore in Corte Madera, California. On the advertisement was a face I instantly recognized. It was Terry Brooks. I knew he came to California often for book signings, so that wasn't a surprise. But that wasn't what the advertisement was for.

Terry was coming to Corte Madera to teach a creative-writing class. It went from nine a.m. to four p.m. on a Saturday in October. Students would submit a sample of their writing to him in advance, and he would give them feedback during the seminar.

My heart began to pound faster with anticipation. All my life I had wanted Terry to read something I'd written.

This was my chance to meet the giant in person and learn from him. To see a view from his shoulders that I had never experienced before.

That class was a turning point moment in my life and career.

But not in the way that I expected.

FEEDBACK—THE PAINFUL GIFT

It wasn't the first time I'd met Terry Brooks. I had attended several book signings previously, where I would stand in line for an hour for a chance to meet him for thirty seconds. This was different, however. He had read my writing. Driving there, my stomach twisted into knots of anxiety. I both looked forward to and dreaded attending his writing seminar. In my car was a duffel bag with all the copies of his books that I owned, including a copy of *Sometimes the Magic Works*.

I drove past San Quentin State Prison to get there. I'm not sure why that memory has stuck with me all these years. Maybe the prison felt like a symbol for the prison of a writer's anxiety . . . the way it threatens to cage our passion with self-doubt? When I pulled into the parking lot and found the classroom, I waited in anticipation for the class to begin. Every member of the class had submitted a writing sample in advance so Terry could read the samples and prepare his thoughts on how to critique them. Of the three fantasy series I was working on at the time (Landmoor, Minya, and Kingmakers), I had decided to submit the prologue of *Tears of Minya*, thinking it was the most polished and represented my best work.

There weren't many of us in the class, probably twelve to fifteen students in all, so it was a rather intimate setting. He lectured for the first bit, and I took a lot of notes, planning to use this experience for an article in *Deep Magic*. Then he began to critique the samples one by one. He read each of them out loud, which I hadn't expected, and proceeded to rip them apart, much like a prosecuting attorney might do to shred the case of his opponent.

Although he hadn't made it to my sample yet, my excitement had quickly transformed into dread. There were very few things he liked about the samples, it seemed, and he pointed out plenty of flaws and discrepancies of logic. He also asked questions of the authors, and their fumbling answers revealed that they hadn't thought things out very far. He wasn't mean. I don't want to give that impression. But the feedback was direct and meant to subdue the budding ogre of author pride inside each of us. His words left everyone feeling humbled, if not a little attacked. Then he got to my piece.

I tried to swallow my pride as I listened to him read my prologue. Thankfully, he didn't rip it to pieces, but he did find fault with it. He made some suggestions and asked some questions about where I was intending to take the story. I explained the prologue's purpose of establishing the protagonist as worthy of readers' interest and admiration. It was backstory, really, but Terry suggested that I further develop the secondary characters. Then he moved on to the next participant.

I certainly felt relieved that he hadn't humbled me in front of everyone else. But I also disagreed with his advice to develop the other characters more because they wouldn't be featured in the rest of the book.

Around noon, we broke for lunch. Many of us ended up in the small café of a bookstore near the classroom. After grabbing lunch at the counter, I noticed a few other students had gathered around a larger table. They were complaining about how ruthless Terry had been, saying they were afraid to go back to his class. Rather than sit with them, I picked a small two-person table and sat down to eat my lunch. Terry entered the café a few minutes later. He glanced around the room, and I imagined he wondered where he was going to sit. I hoped he would sit by me.

If there really is any magic in our thoughts, I must have used mine to sway him. I watched him as he waited for his sandwich and pleaded with him, in my mind, to come sit by me. It was a lot to hope for from someone who had admired him since junior high. He took his tray and started to look for a table. He noticed me, and he noticed the larger group. Both had extra chairs.

He approached my table and asked if he could join me for lunch.

I was so grateful for that little miracle. He sat down, and I told him how much I had enjoyed the class so far. I said we were probably all a little worried about the feedback he would give us, but that's why we had come, and I was grateful he wasn't pulling any punches. He said that pulling punches doesn't help anyone grow. That if you're going to give feedback, it should be honest and with the intention of helping the other person become a better writer. The only way to do that is to be specific about the ways someone's writing can improve.

I've taken that message to heart, and when I give feedback, I try to do the same. What needs to be said to make someone's writing better? But I also realize how sensitive we authors are and that a little "brown sugar" helps the medicine go down.

I don't remember everything we talked about during our lunch together, but he did tell me about his road to publication. You can't just make it happen on your own, he insisted. His journey was almost like fate. He happened to submit to Lester del Rey at the exact time he was launching a new imprint at Random House. Lester took a chance on him. It wasn't predictable—history isn't, of course—and it required a lot of good luck. In fact, it seems to me the first word in the title of his memoir tips its hat to that fact. *Sometimes the Magic Works.* "Sometimes." Like he didn't trust that his creativity would always work all of the time.

The most memorable thing about that lunch was the encouragement he gave me personally. He looked at me across the table and told me I was the best writer in the class. That he saw some raw talent and felt that, should the stars align, he could see me getting a publishing deal someday.

Encouragement goes a long way toward fanning someone's inner spark rather than snuffing it out. I'd learned that first in high school, when that girl asked me about my book, and the lesson has continually repeated itself over the years. Just a few words of kindness can provide fuel that motivates for a long time.

Terry's praise meant the world to me. I'd been on that road to publication for a long time. I'd written many novels, short stories, and articles, as well as academic essays, and even a master's thesis. His kindness helped bolster my courage. I wasn't there yet. But I was getting closer.

During that class, Terry gave us a lot of good advice about how our magic systems should make sense. There should be an internal logic that resonated with the reader and, even more importantly, with us. He taught us that if we don't delve outside our comfort zone, our fiction will become boring. If it's hard to write about, we should write about it. This counsel has helped motivate my own quest, which is why I haven't flinched from taking certain risks (Owen Kiskaddon was only eight in the first Kingfountain book) and leaving behind the worlds I've created to venture into completely new ones, as I do in the Grave Kingdom Series.

But the words he said that resonated with me the most are from the quote he attributed to Stephen King. *After you've written your first million words, then you are ready to* start *being a writer.*

As I've already said, I went home and tallied up my words. I'd nearly reached the one million mark at that point. What did that mean? I had gone to Corte Madera wondering which of my series I was going to focus on for the future. It hadn't occurred to me that the answer was *none* of them. After class, I asked if he would sign my books, and he graciously agreed to sign all of them after everyone else had had their turn. I drove back home with a mixture of feelings. I was so grateful to have had the experience with him, but that quote wouldn't leave my mind. If my first million words had only been practice, would all the previous books I'd written end up unseen?

I was preparing, at that time, to publish the sequel to *Landmoor*. I had intended for it to be my breakout series, one I could continue for many books. I had even promised my readers that it was just the beginning. Maybe I'd been wrong. Maybe, after all the work I'd poured into it, it was time to switch gears.

Change is always around the next corner, and it's usually uncomfortable. This class with Terry was another crossroads moment for me, and trials often come in threes. My family was growing—my wife and I were blessed with a new baby girl—and I was given a new church assignment. I was called in to the bishopric as a counselor to the bishop of our ward. I'd been serving as his executive secretary up to that point. Although it required me to stretch my time across more tasks, I'd made a promise to God that I would serve wherever I was chosen to serve. I had meetings almost every Sunday, starting early in the morning, and then oversaw the twelve-and thirteen-year-old youths in the congregation, the women's organization of the ward, and Sunday school.

Before I had even become acclimated to that new responsibility, I was faced with my third "trial": the group I worked for in Intel was folding. We were told, in November, that we would all need to start looking for a new job within the company by the end of the year.

All of these stresses hit me at the same time. That meant that my time for creative writing, which was already being sucked up by *Deep Magic*, would get even smaller.

If I had to choose where at Intel I wanted to be next, I would have chosen Corporate Real Estate Site Development. It was a rather small group at Intel that had been one of the major internal customers of my current department. I had been a key partner with them and had met many of the managers there. It was a place where I felt my skills would be appreciated.

After learning about the news, I called up one of the managers to see if there might be any possibilities. He was concerned about HR's decision and said that they needed the knowledge we provided. And it turned out that he had an open position on his team. Would I be interested in applying for it?

You can imagine the relief I felt. I shared the news with my wife, and it felt as if heaven was taking care of us. I was absolutely interested in the position. I also looked at other job openings at the site and saw a position for a business operations manager in the IT department. An MBA was required, which I had. But I really wanted a job in CRESD.

I then found out that all job requisitions in Corporate Services, the division that CRESD was part of, had been frozen until further notice. They couldn't hire anyone. The hiring manager pleaded with his vice president to make an exception. Just one exception. They wouldn't do it. The hiring freeze began to grow as executives realized that Intel needed to make some corrections.

If all the open requisitions became frozen, and I was put into redeployment in the new year, it meant that I would likely lose my job. Once again I felt the clock ticking and the pressure to find a seat before the game of musical chairs ended.

Reading the writing on the wall, I decided to apply for the business ops manager job. The hiring manager asked to meet with me immediately. I had the right kind of resumé and the skills for the position, but as I learned about the group, I had no interest at all in joining them. I could do the work, but it would involve managing budgets and going through Intel's financial protocols and helping the managers run staff meetings. They offered me the job almost immediately.

In anguish, I called the manager at CRESD again to see if something could be done. I told him that I had an offer from IT and that if I didn't take it now, it, too, might be frozen, and I'd be stuck without a job during a massive hiring freeze. He did the best he could and appealed again to the VP. The answer was the same. No jobs could be hired until the freeze ended.

I was disappointed to say the least. But I had a family to provide for, as well as obligations at church, so I chose the job in IT. In January of 2005, I changed buildings and went to join my new group. Working at Intel back then basically felt like working on the Death Star. Every cubicle, every carpet tile, and every wall was colored a shade of gray. And in my new cubicle, which was tinier than my previous one, the only window looked out to the side of the neighboring building, which was also a shade of gray. It was a depressing work environment, but I was determined to endure it. At least I had a job.

A few weeks into the new year, my desk phone rang. I saw the name of the hiring manager in CRESD on the screen. When I picked up the phone and answered it, he gave me the good news. The hiring freeze was over. He wanted to offer me the job I'd wanted.

But I had already started my new one.

"It is folly to cross a bridge until you come to it, or to bid the Devil good-morning until you meet him—perfect folly. All is well until the stroke falls, and even then nine times out of ten it is not so bad as anticipated. A wise man is the confirmed optimist."

—Andrew Carnegie, philanthropist, steel tycoon

LOOK UP, THEN BACKWARD

While I was grateful and relieved to hear that the hiring freeze was over, I also knew from my HR experience that Intel had a policy that you can't change jobs after you've accepted one. You have to wait a year before you can apply for another job.

But the manager in CRESD was persistent and felt there was a strong case to be made. He said he would work it out with my manager but wanted to know whether I was still interested in the position. Of course I was—I had wanted the job from the start. I hoped that things would work out and that they could reach an agreement that would allow me to leave early. My new manager in IT talked to me about the situation, confused that I had accepted his opening and wanted to leave so soon, but I think I was able to help him understand that it was a better match for my skills. He said he would consider it and talk to his manager, who was working from India at the time. I knew that me leaving would put them back a few months, but I hoped it wouldn't burn bridges.

The business operations job I'd accepted in IT was definitely not as enjoyable as what I'd done in Staffing Market

Intelligence or what I hoped to do in CRESD. My wife and I prayed that my manager would let me go. And I'll admit that I was confused why things hadn't worked out better earlier. Had I made the wrong decision to go with the IT job? Should I have trusted that things would have turned out better and declined the position?

That's one of the hardest things about life. We cannot see the future. We tend to second-guess ourselves and wring our hands about our choices and options because we don't know how things will turn out. My manager in IT set up a meeting to discuss the outcome of the situation, and I remember going into the conference room with trepidation and a little bit of hope. Yes, I knew Intel had a policy, but I hoped that what was best for the company and for me would align, and I'd be able to join the other team.

You can imagine my disappointment when my boss told me that I would be staying. Even after all the discussion and reasoning, they felt I had an obligation to them for a year and that I should keep that obligation. My stomach sank. I felt terrible. Then he asked if I was going to be professional about the decision and not let the decision impact my performance for the worse. Well, I had already learned the integrity lesson earlier, and I assured him that I understood his position and that I would do my best work for him and make him glad he'd chosen me for the job.

After the meeting, I called my wife at home and told her the outcome. She, too, was disappointed, knowing that I had really hoped it would be different. I was grateful for her compassion and tenderness during such a tense period. I called the hiring manager at CRESD and told him I was sorry that it didn't work out. He was sorry too and said that they'd need to go ahead and fill the position so they wouldn't lose the requisition.

Yes, I was disappointed. But I was determined to do my best and to dazzle my new boss. I helped run staff meetings, prepared presentations, and got to know each of the functional managers in my new group while I tried to find ways to help each of them individually. They were smart, hard-working, and kind people. And while I didn't like the building I was in, I did like the people that I worked with and the other biz ops managers whom I got to know. Within a few months, I had transitioned to 100 percent of the duties, and the man who had hired me went on his two-month sabbatical, so I was helping the director in India run the department.

When faced with setbacks, or outcomes that don't work out, I don't think it's very useful to say "Why me?" or to think of it as some sort of punishment. It's best to look up and recognize that you just don't understand all God has in store for you.

In 1975, a barge struck a bridge in Tasmania, causing a large section of the bridge to collapse. This killed several people, including passengers in four cars that plummeted from the bridge in the dark. An Australian family managed to stop in time, and the driver, the father, tried to wave and warn other drivers of the danger. Some heeded the warning and stopped in time, including a bus full of passengers. We just don't see what is coming ahead, and it pays to listen to warnings from others who have a better view. Since none of us can see the future, we are especially dependent on listening to warnings from God. Even when they don't make sense to us at the time. The very darkness of uncertainty blinds us.

Nine months after working in IT, my phone rang again. It was the hiring manager I knew in CRESD. I answered the call, and he told me that they had held the job open for me and hadn't hired someone to fill it. He asked if I still wanted to come work for him.

I was astounded by the call and said yes, but I had three more months required before I could seek another job. He asked if I would talk to my manager, the one in India, and ask again if I could go early. He said they would hold the job open for me anyway, regardless of the decision, but it wouldn't hurt to ask.

I'd learned a lot during the job, but it wasn't a good fit for my interests. I spoke to the division manager and told him the situation and what had come up. I still really wanted that job, but I was prepared to stay the last three months if required. But he knew I would be leaving after that, so why not work on getting a replacement sooner? We had a good relationship by this point. He'd seen the quality of my work and that I did what I said I would do. I was surprised that he didn't ask for time to think about it. His answer surprised me even more. He told me that *he* was in the process of changing jobs, that another manager would be coming over to manage the team. And so he agreed that I could leave early so the new manager could have his own choice in biz ops managers. He agreed to let me go.

I hadn't seen that coming and was grateful he'd confided in me. I accepted the job in CRESD, and then we opened a requisition to replace me in IT. Interestingly, one of the managers in the group had an interest in learning that role, and he took over the job. The new manager of the division was a capable and good man, and he honored the commitment of his predecessor, even though he really wanted me to stay.

Nine months after starting in IT, I accepted a position in CRESD, the group I'd hoped to join earlier. Once again I had to learn a new language, the vocabulary of real estate, space planning, and the L&C, which stands for Land & Construction—a monthly meeting that CRESD had with the CEO of the company to talk about real estate deals. I left IT before the end of 2005. Within six months, the "bridge" collapsed. Nearly everyone in the department of IT that I had been in lost their jobs due to a major corporate restructuring that happened when Paul Otellini became CEO.

It was as if the car I was driving had managed to get off the road just in time. I felt terrible for my coworkers who were suddenly in redeployment and looking for work elsewhere due to the downsizing. But I was also incredibly grateful that I had gotten the job I'd wanted. I wondered for several years why that experience had happened to me. And that's when I learned the principle of look up and then backward.

For most of the jobs I had while I was at Intel, I had been recruited into the position by someone I'd known in advance. After working in CRESD for a few years, the director left, and the position was filled by the manager of the real estate contracts team, a man named Sunil Das. Not long after he took the job, his biz ops manager decided to leave the group, making a vacancy. While I was visiting Arizona for a group face-to-face, Sunil pulled me aside and told me about the opening. He wanted me to be his biz ops manager, which would give me a staff-level position and greater visibility within the organization, as well as a front row seat during L&C meetings.

He asked if I had ever been a biz ops manager before. And that's when I realized that the little detour in IT had prepared me, years in advance, for a job that I hadn't even known was coming.

Look up and recognize that God knows the details of your life. That those details might seem infinitesimal at times, but they are important. We can't see the future. We don't know what experiences we're going to need that will prepare us for what is ahead. And even though we don't know, when we *look backward* later on, sometimes years later, we can see that He guided us on our path all along the way.

WISDOM

One of the habits I began in 2006 was to research and collect quotes that stood out to me as being very wise. I wanted to collect them, learn from them, in the hopes of becoming wiser myself. Wisdom, I realized, would help me in my job, in my role as a counselor to the bishop in my church, in figuring out the next stage of my writing ambitions, and even as a parent of three children. And it would also help my writing too. I would gather the quotes I found and email them to myself so I might refer to them later.

One of my favorite scriptures regarding wisdom is the Epistle of James, Chapter 1:

> 3 Knowing this, that the trying of your faith
> worketh patience.
>
> 4 But let patience have her perfect work, that ye may
> be perfect and entire, wanting nothing.
>
> 5 If any of you lack wisdom, let him ask of God,
> that giveth to all men liberally, and upbraideth not; and
> it shall be given him.

> 6 But let him ask in faith, nothing wavering. For he that wavereth is like a wave of the sea driven with the wind and tossed.
>
> 7 For let not that man think that he shall receive any thing of the Lord.
>
> 8 A double minded man is unstable in all his ways.

Patience. It can be so hard to achieve, but it's the most valuable of gifts and blessings.

The time had come to shut down *Deep Magic*. Jeremy, Brendon, and I all had careers, kids, and church responsibilities. We had tried to turn the e-zine into a self-funding one so that we could pay the authors, but we learned that people don't like paying for something they're used to getting for free. I also realized that it was eating up all the free time that I had. I was more focused on helping produce a monthly magazine than I was on trying to achieve my goal of becoming a full-time writer. In April of 2006, I started a blog meant to document my writer's journey and provide a way for fans of *Deep Magic* to keep following me after we shut down the e-zine. We wrapped up *Deep Magic* with the June 2006 issue. That was also the month that I announced my intention to write a new fantasy novel. I had taken to heart Terry Brooks's lessons. It was time to start something new—a completely fresh series in which I could leverage everything I'd learned from my mentors and my experience as an editor.

During this year of wisdom seeking, I thought that if I was going to write a fantasy story like the ones I used to read in junior high and high school, I should also learn from the best writers. My marketing research revealed that the majority of readers are female. Most boys turned to video games and movies as they got older, but many girls and women remained strong readers. I decided the "target market" for my new book would be moms and their daughters. This led me to the question of which books had endured the longest in that market? I had loved the Harry Potter series since the first book had come out in 1997, but this was only 2006, and I was looking for fiction that had stood the test of time.

I collected some books by famous authors and decided to read them to study why they'd worked—and continued to work—so well. *Pride and Prejudice* by Jane Austen was on the list. So was *Anne of Green Gables* by L. M. Montgomery and *A Little Princess* by Frances Hodgson Burnett. Since I was working with limited time, I used my daily commute (an hour and a half, combined) to listen to audiobooks. As I listened to these classics, I kept my ears perked for the famous scenes readers still talk about. I'd analyze what the author had done to make the situation—and characters—so compelling. As I did this, I realized that the authors were tapping into certain ideas and concepts that resonated with the human soul. These very different books had certain themes in common. Handling situations with honor. Sacrificing oneself for loved ones.

A hero or heroine with strong integrity.

It was in 2006 that I read another life-changing book. Now, it happens that this book had been sitting on my shelf for a few years, a birthday present from my older brother. The somewhat mercenary title—*Think and Grow Rich*—had turned me off from wanting to read it, but my thinking changed after someone referenced the author on *Larry King Live* one night. The book, it turned out, was about the power of positive thinking. Of controlling your thoughts and focusing them on the things you wanted to achieve. Intrigued by the concept, I decided to give the book a try.

From that book, I learned the author had interviewed and was inspired by Andrew Carnegie, who'd given him letters of reference to business executives at major firms in the early 1900s, including Henry Ford, Thomas Edison, and others. Hill had interviewed them all to learn the laws of success, which he had then published in his book. I was intrigued and fascinated. There were many other writers who also espoused the power of thought, I discovered. I went on to read Carnegie's autobiography, Benjamin Franklin's autobiography, James Allen's *As a Man Thinketh*, and then Dale Carnegie's classic *How to Win Friends & Influence People*.

One of the things I discovered from all these authors and many others was their penchant for reading and learning wisdom from others, especially ancient philosophers. This is when I started reading Ovid, Seneca, Plato, and others. I also read biographies about John Adams, Abraham Lincoln, and Alexander Hamilton, and they, too, talked about gaining their wisdom from the masters of the past just by reading books.

I found myself wondering if I was even *supposed* to be writing. Had I been clinging to a childish dream for too long? Was my hobby really just a way to waste time? The words I'd read in *Freakonomics* still unsettled me from time to time, plus Terry's advice had rattled my confidence a little.

I researched this too, taking a special look—and listen—at past talks given at general conferences of the church. I still have the email I sent myself on April 6, 2006, entitled "Developing Talents/Hobbies." One of the quotes I sent to myself in that email was from Russell M. Nelson: "Hobbies can help in spiritual development. Music, dance, art, and writing are among the creative activities that can enrich the soul. A good hobby can dispel heartache and give zest to life."

After reading that statement, which I agreed with on a personal level, I felt as if I'd received the go-ahead from God to continue pursuing my dream so long as I didn't let it distract me from my other responsibilities.

I began writing my new novel. I was so inspired by the idea of thoughts making things real that I used Hill's premise as the underpinnings of the magic system in *The Wretched of Muirwood*. The wisdom I'd gleaned from these readings inspired the quotes I used in *Wretched* from the tomes studied by the learners of the abbey. The students themselves were, in turn, partially inspired by the teenagers in the seminary class I'd taught.

The more books I read, the more insights began to flow. I started to read about the lives of famous people—a habit that would influence my writing a great deal—and noticed common traits, including persistence, patience, concentration, a hunger for knowledge and books, the art of human relationships, and the tenacity to avoid procrastination. As I applied these learnings to work and church, I found that the advice was sound. People started listening to me and valued my judgment and experience, even though I was only thirty-five.

POSSIBILITY THINKING AND THE POWER OF POSITIVITY

One of the principles that I learned at Intel and have used since then is the idea called possibility thinking. This isn't just a buzzword for out-of-the-box thinking. No, to practice possibility thinking, you have to throw the box away. It requires you to stop thinking in terms of something being impossible to do, but to envision what it would take to make the impossible possible.

For example, let's think about a semiconductor wafer fab. Having worked in one, I knew that it took around forty days for a microchip to go through the process. There were so many rules and regulations about production that improvements were always incremental instead of radical. Then the executive in charge of manufacturing dared to ask the question—what would it take to cut that time in half? I wasn't in the meeting, but I can imagine the people who were there regarded him with skepticism and horror, much like Luke Skywalker clinging to a pole and staring at Darth Vader. *That's not true! That's impossible!*

Well, they tried a few tests to see how fast they could, theoretically, run a wafer nonstop through the factory. Those tests led to valuable information. That information led to more tests. And a few quarters later, the cycle time of running *every* chip through the fab had dropped, roughly, in half.

A book is made up of so many chapters. How long does it take to write a book? What could I do to speed up the process?

Because I had stopped publishing *Deep Magic*, I had a little more free time for writing my new book. After a discussion about my goal with my wife, we set aside Wednesday nights, from seven to ten p.m., as the time I would write. What could I do to make the most of that time? What if I silenced my phone so I wouldn't be distracted by incoming calls or texts? What if I got a white noise machine to help block out my noisy kids? What if I spent more time setting the scene for the next chapter so I was better prepared to write it? What if I prayed for help to get it done faster? I started devoting one full day of my commute to forming the next chapter in my head while I drove instead of listening to an audiobook, which helped me make the most of the time I had.

In order to come up with new ideas, you must stop thinking in terms of what's possible and impossible. If you despair that you'll never find time to write regularly, then here's the honest truth—you won't. Sometimes I would shift which night I wrote because other things came up, but these were rare exceptions, and I always tackled the week's assignment to write a new chapter, even if I did it under not-so-ideal circumstances.

Possibility thinking means no excuses. How can the work be done differently to achieve the goal?

Thinking beyond what's impossible isn't enough, though—you must also envision what *is* possible.

In *Think and Grow Rich*, Napoleon Hill suggested posting a written statement of your goals in a highly visible place and reciting those goals each morning and night. The universe, he claimed, will begin to offer up ideas for how you might achieve your goals.

I did just that. In 2007, I put my goal on PowerPoint and printed it out and taped it to my bathroom mirror, where I could see it every day and repeat it—and the steps it would take to get there—to myself. This is what I wrote:

By July 1, 2008, I will receive an advance of $100,000 for my completed novel, The Wretched of Muirwood, and a contract to publish two sequels. I will spend up to 4 hours a week preparing a publishable manuscript. To do this, I will seek feedback and input from individuals who are in the target market of this book. I will request assistance from copy-editors I know to help assure the highest quality of the manuscript. Through my network of published authors, editors, and agents, I will discover an agent willing to represent me and who will secure the advance and the contract for me.

To make it even more real, I made a photo montage of home offices with smiling authors sitting at their desks. And I made a fake check to myself for $100,000 from Del Rey Books.

In all my previous attempts to get published, I hadn't really tried to get an agent to represent me. This time, I decided, I would do it the "right way"—or so I thought. I enlisted help from my niece, Jenna, who was a teenager at the time, and asked her to read the chapters I wrote each week to make sure my main character, Lia, was realistic and relatable. Then, because I also wanted the story to appeal to adult readers, I enlisted the help of my sister, Emily.

After I finished the first book, I decided to prepare the manuscript to share with agents after soliciting more feedback from early readers. I began pitching to agents whom I discovered online and through *Writer's Market*. I tried several different query letters, but this is the one that ended up getting the best response rate.

Imagine a world where words are so precious they are only etched into gold.

Muirwood Abbey is one of the few places where learners are taught to read and engrave, and thirteen-year-old Lia wants nothing more than to learn. But she is a wretched, a foundling, and doomed to remain in the Aldermaston's kitchen, forbidden to read. Her most realistic future is to prepare recipes in a privileged household when a knight-maston abandons a wounded squire at the kitchen in the middle of the night. When sheriff Almaguer comes hunting for him, their escape forces Lia and the squire – Colvin – into an alliance bringing Lia closer to her dream of reading and Colvin to his fear of a battlefield death or even worse.

THE WRETCHED OF MUIRWOOD is complete at 75,000 words. It is the first book of a YA fantasy series. I am one of the founders of Deep Magic, a fantasy e-zine published from 2002-2006, which enjoyed two thousand monthly readers. Sample issues are on my website. I have interviewed many leading fantasy authors for writing craft articles, so I have been 'tutored' by the likes of Robin Hobb, George R.R. Martin, and Terry Brooks (who also tutored me personally in his writing seminar in Northern California and has read the first chapter and synopsis and offered his advice and encouragement for publishing it).

Thank you for taking the time to consider representing my work.

Kind Regards,

Jeff Wheeler

I finished the book before the end of 2007 and began seriously querying. My goal was to find an agent and secure the deal by mid-2008. Rejection after rejection came in, but occasionally an agent would ask to see a partial manuscript. One of those who requested the full manuscript was a man I'd interviewed for *Deep Magic*.

I worked on the sequel, because I knew the process might take months or years and wanted to continue writing one night a week to keep the words flowing. Creativity can atrophy as an unused muscle does.

In his book *Great By Choice*, Jim Collins teaches the twenty-mile-march principle. He tells the story of two explorers competing to reach the South Pole. One of the teams focuses on just going twenty miles a day, regardless of the weather. On fair days they went twenty miles. On horrific days they went twenty miles. The moral of the story is that those who set reasonable performance goals and stick with them tend to achieve their goals better than those who rely on motivation. I didn't realize it at the time, but my goal of writing one chapter a week, one book a year, was a twenty-mile-march goal. Believe me, it's a lot easier achieving a reasonable goal when you know exactly what it is and what it takes to get it done. The power comes in sticking with it, regardless of circumstances. In fact, your steady pace alters circumstances in your favor. You come across opportunities you might not have found otherwise.

As the months ticked away, bringing me closer and closer to July, I started to seriously doubt that I was going to achieve my goal. But instead of listening to my inner critic, I continued to focus my thoughts on achieving success and landing a publishing contract. What else could I do while I waited?

I also kept writing. Kept listening to more books and analyzing them. Kept reading biographies about successful people. I was more determined than ever to become one myself.

There truly is no pain so awful as that of suspense.

July 2008 came. I hadn't found an agent to represent me. There was no check for $100,000. In all, I believe I had contacted around forty-two agents. I still have the Excel spreadsheet listing all of the agents I'd contacted.

An envelope arrived in the mail shortly afterward from one of the agencies. I picked it up from the mailbox by my house. I stared at it, dreading what it contained. I think I knew that it was a rejection because I figured they would have called me if they'd been interested.

I kept it.

The disappointment was deep. I pulled into the garage and sat there a while, feeling like a failure. I wondered if Hill's work had worked for everyone but me. But if there was one key message I'd gotten from *Think and Grow Rich*, it was this—success was usually right around the corner from failure. Failure is a test to see if you will quit.

I showed the letter to my wife, and she gave me a hug. She still thought *The Wretched of Muirwood* was the best book I'd ever written and very publishable. It wasn't what was popular in fantasy at the time. More and more books were grimdark. I'd seen that trend in the successful books I'd studied. But I'd made a commitment to myself, my family, and God that I would write books that didn't rely on sex, swearing, and gore. Maybe that meant my readership would be pretty small. Maybe I was just too old-fashioned. But I wanted my kids to be able to read my books. I wanted the youths that I'd mentored over the years to be proud of me.

I took my own advice and looked up. I would keep trying. I hadn't stopped writing the sequel and I *wouldn't* stop writing it. My twenty-mile march plodded on. The goal was to publish a trilogy, and so I needed to hold up my end of a nonexistent deal.

August and September passed. I had that nudging feeling again that something crucial was about to change in my life.

Something dramatic was coming. I wasn't sure what it was, but maybe it was the book deal I had wanted.

I was driving home from work when my wife called. With a shaking voice, she said she had just gotten off the phone with someone who'd made a surprising request. In my church, bishops report to the stake presidents, who are responsible for larger geographical areas. At the time, I was just a counselor to the bishop—the fact that the stake president had asked to meet with me likely signaled a big life change was imminent.

In October 2008, the stake president told me that he had felt inspired that I was to become a bishop. I was humbled by both the honor and the responsibility. Having served as a counselor to the bishop for some time, I had an idea of the amount of work and the emotional toll involved. But then he surprised me. I would not be the bishop over the congregation where I lived. The boundaries were being changed, and I would become the bishop of a congregation where 90 percent of the congregants didn't even know who I was. My wife was pregnant with our fifth child, due in March. We had lived in the Sacramento area for seven years, and this was the *second* boundary change because of all the growth that had happened in the city.

Sometimes it takes years to see the why when things don't work out the way you planned or expected. Sometimes it only takes a few months.

If I'd thought I was busy before, things were about to shift into overdrive.

Looking up, I told God it was okay. I would do my best to meet the challenge he'd given me. I realized that my dream of being a published author would need to be postponed until after the assignment was fulfilled, and I was all right with that. I would stop trying to find a publisher so I could focus on my new duties.

I had prayed for wisdom and had gotten more and more opportunities to gain it. I still had no idea what was coming next.

PAIN'S PERSPECTIVE

Becoming a bishop changed me in almost every respect. It's a challenge that you can't really understand unless you experience it. I learned a great many lessons in that role over the five and half years I was in it, but one that has stayed with me ever since is that everyone is in pain over something.

Sometimes the pain is obvious, and everyone knows about it. While I served as a counselor, one of the teenagers in our congregation was struck by a car while riding his bike to high school after seminary one morning. He suffered extensive injuries, including brain swelling so severe that the doctors had to remove part of his skull. We all thought he might die that first weekend. Thankfully, through several miracles that can only be attributed to the power of God, he was eventually healed and was soon back in the congregation. The doctors said he'd suffered so much brain damage that he probably wouldn't be able to talk or walk again. Nope. He did both and went on to serve a mission.

That family's pain was visible to everyone who saw them at church each week. But they weren't alone—I quickly discovered that every single family in my new congregation was dealing with something painful. One of the first things I did as bishop was visit one of the teenagers from my congregation in jail. As a child, I had thought the most important role a bishop played was in conducting meetings and giving talks. The experience of being a bishop taught me differently. The most powerful impact I had in that role was in one-on-one meetings with a person in pain. Even now, when I'm no longer a bishop, I look around at the congregation and wonder what each person is going through. What their story is. Because I have no doubt there is plenty of pain to go around. My perspective has permanently changed—I'm more sensitive to the quiet suffering of others, which has helped me be a better person as well as a better writer. Whereas once I struggled to be a character writer, now I'm better able to tap into the emotional anguish of a situation.

Henry Eyring once said "when you meet someone, treat them as if they were in serious trouble, and you will be right more than half the time."

I've learned this *is* true more than half the time. And if they're not in serious trouble today, they will be there tomorrow. Just wait. This had played out numerous times in my own life.

I've learned that bad decisions can lead to feelings of deep guilt that just do not go away. I once counseled with a widowed lady who had been troubled by her conscience for over forty years because she'd stolen something from a neighbor. The thing she'd taken had absolutely no value, but the memory had tortured her for decades. She'd never even told her husband, who had passed, about the incident. Finally, she came to see me, looking for hope and help. I listened to her and then asked what she thought she might do to set things right. She said the couple she had stolen from was dead now, but that she knew they had some older children in the area. If she wrote them a letter and apologized and then sent them a little bit of money to pay for the thing she had taken, which was really quite trivial—forty dollars as I remember it—then it might be enough. It mortified her to write that letter, but she did it. And she received a gracious response a few weeks later. If the children's parents had known about the theft, they hadn't said a word. There had never been any hard feelings about it. But none of that mattered. The hard feelings were in this sweet woman's heart—only they were all focused on herself.

I saw variations of this pattern repeated over and over. I've experienced it myself countless times. We can put off the day of reckoning, but eventually it catches up. And isn't it wonderful that we don't have to feel guilty forever about mistakes from our past? We can change, repent, and make things right again.

My own mistake from earlier in my career—that awful night I was caught sitting in the hiring manger's chair in Public Affairs—had stayed with me for a long time too. One day, I asked my new boss at Intel why he'd chosen to hire me of all the people who'd applied for the job. He replied that, in addition to my experience, he had wanted me to work for him because of my integrity. He had no idea how much his words meant to me, and here was evidence that people can change, even me!

The last rejection letter I received from an agent came a month before I became bishop. I'd accepted the responsibility of being a bishop of an unknown congregation fully expecting it would require me to put my dreams on hold for years. But dreams have a dogged sort of persistence.

I'd finished writing the second book of the Muirwood series and had started on the third. One chapter a week, one book a year. That was my goal, and I was determined to stick to it. Yes, my life was incredibly busy. My little sister, who read new chapters each week, kept asking if she could share it with people she knew and felt would love it. I was nervous about this, but after being assured that they wouldn't pass it on to anyone else, I began to gradually share it with others. The responses to the Muirwood books were incredibly positive. Those who got to read it also wanted to share it with friends and relatives.

In June of 2009, I wrote myself an email with another idea. I'd tried to find an agent and go the traditional route but had failed. As I'd learned in *Think and Grow Rich*, failure usually meant a new plan was needed. Even though the dot-com era had ended in disaster, the tech industry still thrived. Amazon had released the first Kindle device in November 2007. Social media had also come onto the scene. Things were changing. Evolving. The email I sent myself was a strategy for self-publishing the entire Muirwood trilogy and releasing all three books simultaneously. This was before binge-reading was a thing, but I imagined that if a reader didn't have to wait long between books, they'd be more likely to buy all three. Authors normally took several years in between books, so I might differentiate myself by making books available faster.

I mulled over the idea and then pushed it aside, determined to focus on my current responsibilities and finish writing the third novel, which I did that summer. I had the entire trilogy finished. What was I going to write next? I wanted to stick to my goal of writing one chapter a week, so I decided to write a series set in the world of Mirrowen. I deliberately didn't write more Muirwood books because I didn't want to be a one-trick pony, although I did continue to reread and edit them while working on the new project. I had many worlds within my imagination and wanted the freedom to explore them all. Mirrowen was special to me because it, too, had started with an online D&D campaign with my friends.

I continued to share copies of the Muirwood books privately with my friends and friends of family members. I also blogged occasionally about my experiences and would share some of those posts on social media. One day, a friend of mine from high school contacted me and asked if she could read a sample of my writing. I obliged, sending her the first two books of the Muirwood series, and she inhaled them in just a few days. I still have the email she wrote me, demanding a copy of the third book, even though it wasn't finished at the time. Her encouragement—remember that principle?—made me think there were others who would want to read the series. Maybe I should just move forward with self-publishing it so that people who wanted to read it could.

As we reached the end of 2010, I got an email from CreateSpace, which I had researched as a venue for possibly self-publishing my series. The company had been acquired by Amazon by this point. They offered a discount for producing a print novel, including a complimentary Kindle version. Kindle was still in its infancy at this point. I mulled over the offer and then talked to my wife about it. We'd never recouped the money we'd spent self-publishing any of my books or *Deep Magic*. Here was another expense that might never be paid back. She wasn't being insensitive, but remember that we had a mortgage to pay, plus five little kids. Life had gotten expensive. It would require a sacrifice from our family to do this. But because she was so supportive of my dream, she agreed. I then contacted CreateSpace and asked if they would offer a steeper discount if I published *three* books at once. They did, so that lowered the cost a little bit too.

I promised my wife that I wouldn't pour too much time and energy into trying to market the books. I'd use social media and let word of mouth do the rest. If nothing happened, nothing happened. Part of the CreateSpace package included physical copies of the books, which I intended to give away to friends and family all over the country in the hopes that they'd be loaned out and shared with others, who might then want to buy their own.

It was exciting doing this and took several months to work out the layout, cover art, and formatting with CreateSpace. I got my author copies and began sending them to the people I'd asked to help spread the word. I'd made an e-book version too, and I got a notice from Smashwords that the first copy had sold all on its own. I can't describe how excited that thought made me—someone out there, someone I didn't even know, was reading my book.

A few reviews came up on Amazon, and many kind messages were sent to me on Facebook or by email. But sales were tepid at best. In my heart, I'd hoped for some viral phenomenon to take place, catapulting me to creative-writing stardom. Nope. The reviews were positive in general, and to my delight, strangers were discovering the series too. Each new review was read with great anticipation. Still, it was slow and disappointing. I thought of ways that I could try to market the books, but then remembered that I'd promised my wife I wouldn't expend more resources on the project (time included). We'd let it go where it went.

Reviews and sales began to fizzle out toward the end of the year. I was a little surprised to discover the e-book version sold more than the print version. As the end of the year approached, I again saw the looming signals of failure.

Yet another plan I'd made hadn't worked. Some of the reviews complained about the typographical errors in the books. In order to save costs, I hadn't paid for the line-editing service offered by CreateSpace, trusting in my own editing abilities. I didn't even know about developmental editors back then or that I could hire one. Every time I saw one of those complaints, I grew more discouraged and wished that I had tried to make it more professional. At that point, the books were too familiar to me for me to look at them with an editor's eye.

In December of 2011, while I was on a two-week vacation with my family, I got another email. It was from a fan in Australia who'd read the Muirwood series to her children. They'd all loved the books. Her only complaint was that there were numerous typos in the manuscripts that should have been caught by any decent proofreader. She didn't want to offend me by saying this, but offered to send me an email with all the typos she'd found in the hopes that I'd fix them so that others wouldn't be bothered. I thanked her for her offer and gladly accepted.

During that little respite from work, I spent several hours fixing the typos and errors she'd emailed me from the three books in the series. I had to notify CreateSpace and have them all fixed, which cost extra. That was painful. During that week, I'd spent hours trying to fix the flaws in a manuscript I'd worked hard on for several years.

Once again, I questioned if I had what it took. Maybe I should just accept that I'd be spending the rest of my career at Intel. It wasn't so bad. I liked the people I worked with. I enjoyed the work itself. But sometimes, as I walked from my cubicle to the cafeteria, I would find myself imagining what it would be like if I never had to work there again. How would that feel?

I still wanted to achieve my dream, but was it just a dream? The wish of a teenager who hadn't grown up yet?

Again I remembered the haunting words from Napoleon Hill. That success often masquerades as failure. That when we persist and don't quit, it comes around the corner. But how many corners had I passed over the years?

I finished fixing the manuscript and ordered new copies for myself.

It was during that week in 2012 that I saw Simon Sinek's first TED talk from 2010. In the talk, "How Great Leaders Inspire Action," he describes the importance of knowing *why* we are doing what we're doing. Not the what or the how. The important thing is knowing the why.

Why do we persevere on a worthwhile opportunity when people keep telling us to quit? Why do we want to do what we feel passionate about? Why do we work hour after hour on our first million words, even though no one will ever read all of them? Why do you have a passion for something that you can't explain, even to yourself? Why were you born with a need to do something, to become something, that feels foolish to others but not to you? Why are you willing to sacrifice sleep, or television shows, or social activities to work on it, even when no one else seems to care? Why does this desire to accomplish something drive you to keep pushing forward against a hurricane of opposition?

On January 7, 2012, I wrote an email to myself to articulate my why. Shortly after, I posted it on my blog, even though I had very few followers. It was a cry from my heart. A candle in the darkness.

I called it "A Manifesto on Virtue."

The next chapter is that post.

A MANIFESTO ON VIRTUE

When I was in college, I took Latin classes from Marianina Olcott. That is where I learned about the Roman concept of Virtus (pronounced "where-tuus"). It was a trait that the Romans respected, but it did not mean just *virtue*. It included other qualities too: *prudentia* (prudence), *iustitia* (justice), *temperantia* (self-control), and *fortitudo* (courage).

As I look around in the world today, I see that these traits are no longer honored and respected as they were in the past. Maybe that is why I love reading and why I have certain favorite movies I watch over and over again. You see, in my favorite books and films, the stories that grab me are about Virtus. All right, they can be cheesy sometimes. But I love that moment in *Return of the Jedi* when Luke throws down his light saber and tells the emperor he failed to turn him to the Dark Side. That despite everything that will happen to his friends and (gulp) his "sister," he surrenders and takes the blast of Force lightning full in the chest. That is Virtus.

I'm also a huge fan of the classics for the same reason. Victor Hugo's *Les Misérables* grips me because Jean Valjean gives up a comfortable career, a position of respect as a mayor, after struggling for years to escape his criminal past. And he gives it up because another man was accused in his place. The rest of his life is devoted to safeguarding a child he does not truly bear any responsibility for. That is Virtus.

Virtus may have been seen as a manly quality in ancient Rome, but it isn't limited in my mind. All of my favorite characters demonstrate it. Jane Eyre leaves Edward Rochester after learning he has a wife, despite his urgent pleas for her to forsake her morals. "Laws and principles are not for the times when there is no temptation; they are for such moments as this, when body and soul rise in mutiny against their rigour; stringent are they; inviolate they shall be. If at my individual convenience I might break them, what would be their worth?"

It is Samwise Gamgee bearing Frodo up the mountain on his back, refusing to abandon his friend. It is the Elven girl Amberle being willing to give her life to save a people who hates her and the humble healer Wil Ohmsford protecting her along the journey at great personal cost.

As I have studied biographies of some of the great ones in history, I have found many examples of Virtus echoed through the ages. They are not perfect people. They are always rare.

The problem is, they are becoming even more rare. As I read many of the popular books in the genre I love, I can hardly find any trace of Virtus left. Sure, there is a spattering appearance of it now and again, but the core of the story and the general plots are thick with meaningless violence, no self-control to speak of, and heroes so flawed I am not sure I even want them to succeed.

In the world I live in, there are plenty of harsh realities. But when I want to enjoy a movie or delve into a book, I want to be inspired. I want to see someone rise to the challenges instead of submit to them. I want to see more Virtus. I want to cheer for Eliza Bennett when she realizes the man she despises the most is the one who's just right for her. I want Taran the pig-keeper and Eilonwy to stay behind and heal the world of Prydain instead of sailing off to a fair country. I want to cry when Harry goes into the Forbidden Forest alone with his ghosts.

Virtus isn't about being a supercool vampire with too much time and money on his hands. It is about trying to be someone bigger than yourself despite the odds being stacked against you. It is about falling down, getting scuffed up, and getting right back up again. Even when the one you love goes another way. Even when you fail sometimes.

That is what I like to read and watch.

And that is why I write.

THE "GUH" MOMENT

When I'd decided to self-publish the Muirwood series, I sold it through Smashwords so that I could hit as many e-book platforms as possible. Since I also had a Kindle Direct account, I received an email notification about a new marketing opportunity they were testing. If I made my books available through KDP exclusively for three months, they would allow me to give away my books for free for a few days.

I still remember getting that email and thinking—*what could it hurt?* The exclusivity clause was only three months, and if sales suffered, I could always switch back at the end of the period. After consulting with my wife, we decided to sign up all three books in the series for the deal, but we'd test out the free promotion on just the first book. To be honest, so much was going on in my life that I forgot I'd signed up for it.

It wasn't until the following week that I began to notice that the number of reviews on Goodreads had ticked up quite a bit after remaining at a plateau for a long time. I had no idea who these people were. Then I got an email invitation to be featured in a blog. Finally I remembered that I had signed up for the program. It had been over a week since it had happened.

The kids were in bed, and I got on my laptop in the den. I opened up the browser and went to the website to check the sales dashboard. What I saw astonished me. At first I thought it was a typo. I was so shocked that I took a screenshot of it because I couldn't believe it.

In two days, I'd given away 10,577 copies of the first book. In the same reporting period, less than 60 copies of the other two books had sold, so that meant over 10,000 copies had come from the KDP promotion. Yes, they'd been freebies. But I'd never seen numbers anywhere close to that for anything I'd published previously.

I refreshed the browser, wondering if it was an error. The same screen came up. I babbled my wife's name as I ran to the kitchen. Were my eyes deceiving me? I couldn't get any words out, and when she saw me, she may have been alarmed that I was experiencing a stroke, because I kept saying "guh!" over and over and gesturing for her to come with me.

I led the way back into the den, slumped down in my chair, pointed at the screen, and said it again. *"Guh!"*

She looked at the number, blinked, and then started hugging me, jumping up and down, and crying all at the same time.

It was the turning point moment, although I didn't know that for sure at the time. But it felt different. It felt amazing.

Over the next few days, I watched as the sales numbers for the second and third books began to jump up as the binge-reading phenomenon kicked in. Some people liked to binge-watch shows on Netflix, and some preferred to start reading a book series after it was completely done. My new readers had gotten a taste of the story and my writing style, and they wanted to know what happened next. In my opinion, the second book was much more intense and interesting than the debut anyway, and once they'd read the first two, they had to know how the trilogy ended. The number of reviews continued to spike on Amazon and Goodreads. And so did the sales for the books at the regular price. Yes, I'd given away a lot of books, but I began to sell more than I ever had previously.

I hadn't used up all the freebies I was entitled to yet with the program, so I decided to give the entire trilogy away for free in February of 2012, just to see what would happen. That month, over 45,000 free copies were given away. You might think this is a bad thing, but it's not. Over the first six months of 2012, I also *sold* over 40,000 books. The royalties I earned during that period more than paid for the publishing costs for everything I'd self-published previously since *The Wishing Lantern*.

Most people are reluctant to part with their money for something unknown. Hence the power of giving away samples. To my mind, word of mouth is the most powerful way books are sold. If readers like a book, they'll buy more. If they love it, they'll tell others. Although I'd known this principle was true for some time, it didn't work for *Landmoor*. I was limited then by the existing readers for *Deep Magic*. The KDP program had allowed me to reach a much larger and more varied audience.

There are other interesting lessons I learned in this critical phase. The development of good portable e-readers, especially the Kindle device, was a game changer in the publishing industry. Remember, e-readers didn't even exist in the commercial market until the end of 2007. That was only ten years after Amazon went public. The KDP program caused an earthquake in the self-publishing business, one that was felt throughout the publishing world. I happened to be right at the epicenter of the tsunami that followed. My books were on the market at exactly the right time to ride the wave.

I didn't plan any of this, nor did I know it was going to happen. But I do remember feeling those little personal nudges from God—whispers—to start self-publishing the entire trilogy. If I hadn't followed that guidance when I did, the outcome might have been very different. And remember that week around Christmas that I spent editing all the typos out of the trilogy? That happened exactly before things started to go big. It's not a coincidence. And my Manifesto on Virtue? Was that happenstance as well? It was my declaration of what I stood for and what I was going to write during my career. And I believe that upholding the promise I made to myself (and my family and God) has also contributed to my success.

A few months later, in April 2012, I was in my cubicle on the phone with a coworker talking about something work related. An email alert from my Gmail account flashed on the screen with the subject line: *Wretched of Muirwood*.

I'd started getting fan mail by this point, which was always a gift, so while I was on the phone, I toggled over to my Gmail account to read the message. It was from a guy I'd never heard of before, David Pomerico. I was struck immediately that it wasn't fan mail. David was an acquisition editor at 47North, Amazon's new science-fiction and fantasy imprint. I read his email expressing his love for the book, and he said he'd like to talk with me about acquiring it and discussing my next plans.

Needless to say, I had another *Guh!* moment.

I forwarded the email to my wife, while still on the phone with my colleague, who had no idea I was actually having a transcendent experience. She wrote back the following words:

Holy. Cow. Trying not to freak out here. Okay……let's take a deeeeeeeeeeep breath! This sounds so amazing, but heck why jump on the first boat if it isn't a good deal? I can't wait to hear what this man has to say/offer.

WOOOOOOOOOOOOOOOOOOOOOOOOOOHO OOOOOOOOOOOOOOOOOOOOOOOOOOOO!!!!!

Congrats, sweetie! So proud of you….for NEVER giving up. I'd call you right now but I don't know if you have mtgs…

I didn't want to come off as overly eager, so I deliberately waited until the next day before crafting my calm and casual reply to Mr. Pomerico at 47North. Any aspiring writer knows that in actuality, I was anything but calm and collected on the inside. After doing some research on him and the publisher, I learned that David had previously worked for Del Rey Books, which was the publisher I had wanted to work with the most. It was incredibly validating.

We had a quick conference call soon afterward, and I learned more about Amazon Publishing. I hadn't even heard they'd launched a publishing company, largely because 47North had just been "born" on October 11, 2011. While I wasn't the first author they'd signed, I was David's first author since leaving Del Rey and moving to Seattle. He told me, and has told me since, that my Muirwood books reminded him of the classic fantasy he'd fallen in love with as a teenager—Brooks, Eddings, and the like. He thought the world was overdue for what he called "entry-level" fantasy . . . the kind of books a family could enjoy together and that would ignite a new generation of fans.

If I signed with 47North, my books might not make it into traditional bookstores because they were in competition with Amazon. But my publisher would make print, audio, and e-book versions. Having an audiobook was really important to me because of how many I listened to during my commute to Intel each day. When David learned I was working on another trilogy that was set in a totally different world, he offered me a six-book deal. The first three Muirwood books as well as the next three fantasy books I was writing at the time, which ended up being the Whispers from Mirrowen Trilogy.

Here's another strange happenstance that occurred around this time. I met someone at church, an attorney who was interested in writing. We'd become Facebook friends, and he noticed I was starting to get some visibility. He offered to take me out to lunch to talk about writing and publishing. We met down the street from the Intel campus at Chili's. During our conversation, he mentioned a publishing-rights attorney he knew and followed on Twitter. I'd never heard of the man before.

Shortly after that lunch, I was offered a contract with Amazon Publishing, and I needed to hire that rights attorney to help make sure I understood the terms of the contract and the commitment I was making.

I highly encourage seeking professional advice from experts in the industry. While the attorney didn't negotiate my contract for me, he helped me understand that the terms and conditions were generous and just as good as what I would have gotten if I'd landed a publisher with the Big Five—which are the major publishers today: Hachette, HarperCollins, Macmillan, Penguin Random House, and Simon & Schuster.

As David and I spoke about the contract and our future partnership, I told him that I was looking to create a long-term relationship with a publisher. And that I was really interested in a publisher that wanted to innovate within the industry. It was a perfect match. No one could question that the team at Amazon were innovators, and there wouldn't be book-signing tours, which would have impacted my job at Intel as well as my role as a bishop and father.

While we were on the phone, I asked David if I should try to get a literary agent and whether he could recommend any. I could hear the smile in his voice. He said that just about any agent would want to work with me now that I had a publishing contract in hand. But he reminded me that the purpose of an agent was to facilitate the conversation that we were already having. He said it was totally up to me and that he could recommend some good ones if I wanted.

I'd gone that far without one. I decided I'd keep on going.

I signed that contract on June 27, 2012, almost four years after the goal I'd set. What I hadn't known back then was that my publisher was yet to exist.

"Predicting rain doesn't count. Building arks does."

—Warren Buffett, the "Oracle of Omaha"

UNFORESEEABLE

Returning to the question I asked earlier: What would *you* dare to do if you knew you would eventually succeed? Would you wait until tomorrow to start trying? Or would you begin today?

I believe you have it in you to succeed. You were born with the right qualities at the right time in the right circumstances. You were put on this earth to achieve a purpose. It's not easy, but it *is* doable.

Just remember what "success" is. It isn't a six-book contract or a six-figure contract. It isn't a spot on a bestseller list. It isn't the Olympics or the World Cup. It isn't an Academy Award. People mistake success for fame or wealth—the attainment of popularity or profit. I can see why they think that. We've programmed ourselves in society to define it in such a way. And if we never achieve wealth and fame, we consider ourselves failures.

Success means achieving your mission. The word comes from the Latin *succedere*, which is from the root meaning "to climb, to mount, to ascend." Success means you meant to climb something and made it to the top. It means hard work and persistence and achieving your goal. And what is your goal?

It's what you were sent here to do, to become. And you have no idea how amazing it will be. The reason you've suffered so many setbacks—bullying and imposter syndrome and words that accuse—is because something new and interesting and bright will appear in the dark world should you succeed. And darkness can't abide the light and always tries to extinguish it.

While this book is partly about my story and how I accomplished my goal of becoming a published writer, it's also about you. It's about the steps you need to take to pursue your dream. It's about the character you need to develop. It's about the resilience and stubbornness required to achieve it. Because you were meant to do something important. And all your life you will be told you shouldn't even try.

You cannot see your future any more than I could. But what if you could create the future? I'd argue that you can. That you begin to with every good habit you put into practice, every goal you set and meet, and every spark of belief you foster in yourself.

Each year, my wife and I like to work on setting goals for the next year, five years, and ten years. After getting my publishing contract with 47North, I knew I couldn't see the future. I had no idea how things would turn out, so I wasn't ready to quit my job at Intel yet.

But I set it as a five-year goal. One night my wife and I shared our goals as we sat eating ice cream on our date night. When she saw mine, to leave Intel and write full-time, she looked at me as if I were nuts. "In five years? Are you serious?

We have five kids we need to put through college. You are still a bishop. You have a great career at Intel. Are you sure?"

We discussed what we'd need to do to prepare for that possibility, although we couldn't predict whether it would be possible without knowing some real numbers. The books wouldn't release until the following year, 2013. In the meantime, 47North had its hands full. They needed to produce four of my books simultaneously—the original Muirwood trilogy plus the first book in the Mirrowen series, *Fireblood*. They decided to republish Muirwood in January 2013 and then launch the new series in February. Prior to the release, they said I could promote the books all I wanted—they wouldn't start marketing them until the new covers, editing, and audio was done.

I continued to write one night a week, one chapter a week, because I had a contract to deliver the next two books by a certain date. This was definitely a stressful time in my life, and my health did suffer from the weight of the many responsibilities I was juggling. And my oldest child was just becoming a teenager at the time, so parenthood became a new challenge too.

David warned me that sales for Muirwood might have run their course. I shouldn't have high expectations for their rerelease. 47North's marketing would be focusing more on the *Fireblood* launch since it was new material.

When January 2013 came and all the engines began to run, we were stunned by the reception. It wasn't over at all. In fact, things were just beginning for Muirwood, and when the new Mirrowen series launched, its performance paled in comparison to Muirwood on every metric. The sea had changed, and we were all living in a new world as more and more people bought Kindle devices and began to consume electronic books—and talk about them online. Word of mouth is still the most powerful force in making a book popular.

Why did Muirwood click so much with readers? I think it was because the characters are so relatable. The lessons I'd learned from pushing myself to become a character author and not just a plot author had paid off. Human quirks resonate with readers, like Lia's fascination with only the blotchy-skinned apples from the Cider Orchard. I've had many readers tell me that they stop and smell apples before buying them because of her.

I continued to write my new series, but as I came closer to the end of the trilogy, I found myself facing a decision. My royalties now exceeded my income at Intel, and my five-year plan began to look more realistic after all. That's when David and I started talking about what would come next. Because of the excitement still buzzing around the Muirwood series, I thought it might be wise to continue writing in that world for another trilogy. I think it was also apparent, to both of us, that releasing three books in quick succession triggered the binge-reading effect. If I continued to write only one book a year, would that enthusiasm wane?

After I finished book three of Mirrowen, I discussed the proposal for the Covenant of Muirwood Trilogy. With a twist. Instead of publishing the books one year apart, we'd publish them one month apart. This meant I would have to write the entire series in a year to hit the publishing milestones on time. The only way to do that would be if I left Intel and pursued my writing career full-time. This wasn't a decision I made lightly. It came after many discussions with my wife, which included Excel spreadsheet analysis about whether my new career would cover our living expenses.

It was during the contract phase for the Covenant series that I learned David would be leaving Amazon Publishing and heading back to New York to work at another publisher. This created a whole spectrum of uncertainty. Should I stay with APub? Should I stay with David? Did I really need an agent after all?

Thankfully, I met David's replacement, Jason Kirk, and he assured me that 47North was still very interested in a future partnership with me. We continued the contract discussions, and I informed my boss at Intel that I was planning to retire early and would leave in July 2014. If the publishing thing didn't work out, I knew I could always come back to the tech industry and find another job.

That July, I worked my last week at Intel. One of the traditions I enjoyed there was Take Your Kid To Work Day. I got to spend one last day with all my kids at work. We had activities, ate from the cafeteria, and some of my kids even participated in the talent show.

That was the month I became a full-time author. One month later, I was released as bishop of my congregation. Things had totally changed in just a few short weeks. I could hardly believe both occurrences had happened at once.

But things happen in threes, right? Do you want to know what my next assignment was?

I was asked to teach early morning seminary again. How could I say no to several more years of really early mornings? For the crust of bread I'd offered during the years, I'd gotten an entire loaf in return. My dream job. The career I'd wanted since high school.

In March 2018 I was asked by 47North to attend Emerald City Comic Con in Seattle so I could be on a panel with Terry Brooks, Robin Hobb, and Tamora Pierce. Just the four of us. I hadn't seen Terry since taking his class in Corte Madera, but he recognized me. I had sent him a letter and a signed copy of *Wretched* after it was published by 47North, wanting him to know how much his class had meant to me. And now here we were on a panel together, author to author. My appreciation and gratitude for his advice and wisdom burned in my chest. After all, it was in his class that I'd learned about the first million words principle.

I couldn't have foreseen where I'd end up. Not all the job changes at Intel. Not all the self-publishing twists and turns before finding my soul-mate publisher. Ultimately, I achieved more than I'd ever thought possible. I've hit the *Wall Street Journal* bestseller list multiple times.

You will also not be able to foresee the bends in your life. In my opinion, we're not meant to.

This book is, in part, about my journey to becoming a full-time author. How I came to write my first million words and landed my first publishing deal. But the story isn't over yet. Becoming a full-time author has taught me a number of lessons—things I wished I'd known before signing that first publishing deal. I still would have done it, don't get me wrong. But experience is the thing you get just after the time you need it most.

I'm a fan of Napoleon Hill and positive thinking still. But I've discovered that success has dangers all its own. Perhaps this will be the topic of my next nonfiction book. What do you do *after* you've accomplished what you set out to do? How do you avoid the pitfalls and traps that have knocked down the mightiest in their fields?

There's an important thing to understand about your inner critic, the voice telling you that you don't belong. That you're not good enough. As I mentioned at the beginning of this book, success doesn't silence that voice. It only changes the words it uses.

"What is allowed us is disagreeable, what is denied us causes us intense desire."

—Ovid, Roman philosopher

HOW TO SUCCEED

The advice I've heard the most about how to succeed in writing is generally this: read a lot, write a lot, and don't quit. It's pretty easy to remember the three, and I don't disagree with this advice. The problem with its simplicity is that it tells you the how and not the why. It ignores the driving force within us that not only compels us but enables us to do all three.

In this final chapter, I want to summarize many of the principles we've been discussing. There is not one road to success. There isn't an equation you can follow to achieve the outcome you're seeking. In fact, timing can be the most critical (and unpredictable) element of all. Even so, I'm confident that if you follow certain principles, you will achieve the personal transformation you desire. Napoleon Hill said that thoughts become things. Remember what the little train said in the children's book *The Little Engine That Could*? "I think I can. I think I can. I think I can." All I would say is it needs a few extra periods. "I think. I can. I think. I can. I think. I can." Each plan followed by action brings you closer to your goal.

One of the first principles discussed in this book is that you must want the consequences of what you want. Think it through. Do you want to be a writer? An actor? An accountant? What do you want? And are you sure you want it? At first I wanted to be a high school teacher because I thought it would give me time to write. But I enjoyed college more than I did high school, so I shifted my focus to becoming a college professor. That goal changed too, once I got a better sense of what working in academia would require. Maybe it's just the *idea* of a profession that sounds interesting to you. Sometimes learning more about what you set out to do will convince you that you actually want to do something else altogether.

Even when you do get what you want, and it's awesome in many ways, there will always be bumps along the road. Do you think it would be cool to attend a book signing? I did. Until I realized you spend most of it sitting by yourself, especially when you're first starting out. I did a book signing once with Robin Hobb and watched people line up to see her. Hardly anyone came to see me. That's pretty normal. At that same event, I met Patrick Rothfuss, who offered some poignant advice to me when he handed me a bottle of hand sanitizer. "You're gonna need that" was all he said.

I interviewed George R. R. Martin during the early days of *Deep Magic*, long before he became world famous, and I got to have dinner with him in Spokane along with some other Amazon Publishing authors. I heard him say how much he misses being an ordinary guy who could go to a convention and not get mobbed. He had achieved both fame and fortune. He liked the fortune part very well, but felt the weight of his readers' expectations as well as the pressures that came from the show.

Do you know what you want, or do you only *think* you know what you want? Have you thought through what the consequences are?

Have you thought about what it will take to achieve your goal? In this book, we've talked about the first million words challenge. Or it could be ten thousand hours. Are you ready to put in the practice necessary to become successful? What are you willing to sacrifice to get the time? Will you sacrifice time you spend with your family? Your friends? Are you willing to sacrifice sleep to get up earlier to accomplish everything you need to do in your life? Are you willing to go to bed early, as Benjamin Franklin suggested—early to bed, early to rise, makes a man healthy, wealthy, and wise? Years after training myself to be an early riser, I listened to a commencement speech by Admiral William H. McRaven delivered in May 2014 talking about making your bed as the first thing you do when you get up. It's a great speech and great advice for developing mastery of your habits. I'd been doing it for decades by the time I heard that talk.

If you want to perform at a professional level, are you willing to do what it takes to *learn* how to compete at that level? Good intentions don't make the grade. Looking back at my journey, I realize that I learned many, many things from all those years I spent trying to publish books. I published a magazine for four years to learn and to see with an editor's eyes. What are you willing to do to achieve the perspective you need? To see what you need to see?

All of this requires a lot of intrinsic motivation and willpower. But those are muscles that can be developed by setting specific goals and working on them. Creativity is also a muscle. The only way to make it bigger is to give it a regular workout. It might also mean not listening to the negative influences in your life that fuel your imposter syndrome. This may mean shutting out the voices of naysaying family members. It may mean trying to counter negative thoughts inside your own head. Set a goal, and stick to it. I write three chapters a week. Period. End of story. No excuses.

Let's assume you have enough motivation to start. How can you ensure you'll go the distance?

You measure it and break it up into realistic chunks. Make whatever you're doing a consistent habit. You don't have to do much each day. Just figure out what your goal needs to be and then break it down. How many words will you write in a day? Or in a week? If you want to be a concert pianist, how much time do you think that will require? If you're unwilling to put in that time, you won't achieve your goal. Whatever your dream is, figure out what you need to do to achieve it and then plot out your path. If you want to be a writer, it will take around one million words of practice. Do the math. How long are you willing to work on that? As you practice more, as you flex those creative muscles, you'll find there are ways you can become more efficient at doing it.

While you are working on your goal, you still need to feed your brain. You need to learn. In any profession, there are sources available that can teach us. Read books about the people you admire and want to learn from. Take notes. Learn the skill of concentration. Don't just read books about your intended profession but about other areas too. Be curious about the world. Creativity comes when you make connections between things others haven't discovered yet. Read biographies to learn about character development. Read business books to learn about industries. Read stories written by masters of the craft, and analyze them and dissect them. What would have happened in Frances Hodgson Burnett's book *A Little Princess* if Sara's father hadn't speculated in diamond mines and ruined her life? What if she'd grown up spoiled and pampered? It wouldn't have been a very interesting story. What if Elizabeth and Darcy had danced that first night and fallen in love immediately? Then we wouldn't have *Pride and Prejudice*. Peel back the layers of stories. Ask questions. Why do these works still resonate so many years after they were published?

I won't tell you all the lessons I learned doing this. That would deprive you of figuring it out for yourself. And you might discover things that I failed to see. When a new book becomes really popular, I like to grab a copy so I can dissect and analyze it. What emotions is the author conjuring? How did they succeed in doing so? What truths did they uncover, and how can I leverage that truth in my own writing?

How many books can you squeeze into your busy life? Do you listen while on the go? Do you bring books on your phone or device so you can read while waiting for an oil change? Take notes about the points that strike you, or email the ideas to yourself so you can review them later. Doing this will help you retain the information. This might even happen while watching a movie. When a good idea strikes, write it down.

The most difficult part of all of this is the last part. Whatever form it takes, creating can be fun and has its own rewards. Once you get into a flow state, the words (or whatever) just come gushing out. Research is fun too once you've learned to concentrate and train yourself to notice important details.

The hardest part is patience. It is enduring the bouts of loneliness and depression that come when success is (and it will be) elusive. It's especially difficult when you try your best and fail. The temptation will always be to quit trying. Realize that when setbacks happen, and they will, you need to look up first. And then look back to see what lessons may be taught through the advantage of hindsight. There are bridges in front of you. Sometimes they fall. You cannot see what lies ahead. Keep going, watching for indicators and the writing on the wall. Trust in the little voice that guides and directs you, not the one that demeans you and your efforts. Even if you crash, realize that there are things you needed to learn from that period that may be applicable later on.

I will leave you with one last piece of advice to help you on your journey. In the many interviews I've given, podcasts I've been on, and classes I've taught, there is one thing about the craft that I have always been most reluctant to share. It is, by far, the most important piece of advice I can give, but I was reluctant for years to share it because I was afraid of how it sounded. It wasn't until I read Steven Pressfield's amazing book *The War of Art* that I finally got the courage to talk about it, because he did. And if a retired marine can tout the virtues of prayer, then so can a retired bishop!

I think one of the most important decisions I made in my writing journey was asking God to help me out. Because my life was so busy with competing commitments, I felt almost desperate at times with exhaustion, mental fatigue, and emotional crises. When it was time to start writing, I'd kneel down first. I'd ask for help writing faster that night so I could go to bed at a reasonable hour. That action became an important habit. I still do it today. Every time.

I'll leave you with one more quote, a scripture you may or may not recognize. Jesus, the night of the Last Supper, went with his disciples to the garden of Gethsemane. This was before the trial, the scourging ordered by Pilate, and his crucifixion on the hill Golgatha.

> Luke 22:
>
> 41 And he was withdrawn from them about a stone's cast, and kneeled down, and prayed,
>
> 42 Saying, Father, if thou be willing, remove this cup from me: nevertheless not my will, but thine, be done.
>
> 43 And there appeared an angel unto him from heaven, strengthening him.
>
> 44 And being in an agony he prayed more earnestly: and his sweat was as it were great drops of blood falling down to the ground.

In these words, you see prayer mentioned twice. Gethsemane was a very somber setting, a place of ancient olive trees and presses where the fruit was crushed into oil. But what strikes me from these verses is how prayer was used. There was a task to be performed. A mission to be fulfilled. Was there any way it could be avoided? No. But look closer. In answer to the prayer, help came. An angel appeared from heaven, strengthening him. And when things became even more intense, with the awful realization that the cup wouldn't pass, what happened next?

Another prayer. An even more earnest one.

Whatever your goal is in life, whatever it is that you were sent here to do, you were not intended to do it alone.

Help will be given to us if we ask for it. Maybe it's a little wisdom that we need. Maybe it is a mentor. Opportunities come in many disguises. Keep your eyes open so you can recognize them when they come. They won't always make sense at first but probably will later. The key is to act on them anyway to find out what they will teach you.

I know you can do it!

BOOKS ON THE CRAFT

Becoming a Writer by Dorothea Brande
On Writing by Stephen King
Sometimes the Magic Works by Terry Brooks
The War of Art by Steven Pressfield
Creativity, Inc. by Ed Catmull
Made to Stick by Chip Heath & Dan Heath

BOOKS WITH BIG IDEAS

Think and Grow Rich by Napoleon Hill
Outwitting the Devil by Napoleon Hill
As a Man Thinketh by James Allen
Boyd by Robert Coram
How to Win Friends & Influence People by Dale Carnegie
The Greatest Salesman in the World by Og Mandino
The Greatest Miracle in the World by Og Mandino
Leadership and Self-Deception by the Arbinger Institute
Great by Choice by Jim Collins and Morten T. Hansen
The Five Dysfunctions of a Team by Patrick Lencioni
The Innovator's Dilemma by Clayton M. Christensen
Only the Paranoid Survive by Andrew S. Grove
The World of Flat by Thomas L. Friedman
Switch by Chip Heath & Dan Heath
How We Decide by Jonah Lehrer
Willpower by Roy F Baumeister & John Tierney
The How of Happiness by Sonja Lyubomirsky

The Varieties of Religious Experience by William James
10% Happier by Dan Harris
Man's Search for Meaning by Viktor E. Frankl
Predictably Irrational by Dan Ariely
The Power of Habit by Charles Duhigg
Start with Why by Simon Sinek
Factfulness by Hans Rosling
Tools of Titans by Tim Ferriss
Norwegian Wood: Chopping, Stacking, and Drying Wood the Scandinavian Way by Lars Mytting

FAVORITE BIOGRAPHIES

Lincoln by David Herbert Donald
Team of Rivals by Doris Kearns Goodwin
John Adams by David McCullough
Alexander Hamilton by Ron Chernow
Titan: The Life of John D. Rockefeller, Sr. by Ron Chernow
Napoleon by Andrew Roberts
His Excellency: George Washington by Joseph J. Ellis
Benjamin Franklin by Walter Isaacson
Steve Jobs by Walter Isaacson
Einstein by Walter Isaacson
Boyd by Robert Coram
Call Sign Chaos by Jim Mattis
American Lion: Andrew Jackson in the White House by Jon Meacham
Walt Disney by Neal Gabler

ACKNOWLEDGMENTS

I get asked for writing advice a lot, or about what I would have done differently knowing what I know now. The answer I typically give, whether someone is going to go the agent route or the self-publishing route, is to find a good dev editor. I didn't even know they existed until I got my contract with 47North, but I can't imagine writing a book, even this one, without the expert advice and help they bring.

So I'd like to thank Angela Polidoro, my amazing dev editor, for her support over many years and many series and for taking the time to provide feedback and suggestions for this book too. What sets a good dev editor apart from copyeditors or proofreaders, in my opinion, is that they can not only get into the heads of potential readers, but they get into the author's head as well. In many cases, she's helped me rethink my intentions or offered suggestions that fit so well within the worlds I create.

I'd also like to thank, again, David Pomerico, who is now with Harper Voyager. He's my hero. He's the one who made my vision a reality. I'm happy to say that we're still friends and have had chances to meet each other at conventions and my other trips to New York.

I'd like to thank my wife, Gina, for sticking with me, even though, when I was a foolish teenager, I stuck a piece of packing tape on her back at work and she didn't notice it for several hours. I deserved her wrath when she finally found out. I think I've made it up to her by now. Her wisdom and counsel has enabled me to learn from my mistakes, and her unconditional love has supported me during some really hard times.

There are so many others who have supported me over the years, by being first readers, partners in *Deep Magic*, and friends, that I can't name them all. So I'll just conclude by thanking you. You have also been a part of my writer's journey. Yes, you. I may not know your name or your circumstances, but I wouldn't have been able to write this book without you. Thank you for supporting me. Thank you for reading. Thank you for telling people about my books.

I'll try to always live up to your trust.

—Jeff